Tales *of the* Dancing Dragon

Tales *of the* Dancing Dragon

Stories of the Tao

Eva Wong

SHAMBHALA
Boston & London
2007

Shambhala Publications, Inc.
Horticultural Hall
300 Massachusetts Avenue
Boston, Massachusetts 02115
www.shambhala.com

9 8 7 6 5 4 3 2 1

First Edition
Printed in the United States of America

⊗This edition is printed on acid-free paper that meets the
American National Standards Institute z39.48 Standard.
Distributed in the United States by Random House, Inc.,
and in Canada by Random House of Canada Ltd

Designed by James D. Skatges

Library of Congress Cataloging-in-Publication Data
Wong, Eva, 1951–
Tales of the dancing dragon: stories of the Tao/Eva Wong.
—1st Shambhala ed.
p. cm.
ISBN-13: 978-1-59030-523-2 (pbk.: alk. paper)
1. Taoism—China—History.   I. Title.
II. Title: Stories of the Tao.
BL1910.W67 2007
299.5'1409—dc22
2007015601

Contents

Contents

Introduction

Between the black and white of fact and fiction is the vast and colorful realm of legends, sagas, and heroic epics—a region so rich that neither historical fact nor fantasized fiction can capture or reveal it. Growing up in a culture that has a deep sense of historical continuity, I was immersed in the world of historical legends early in my life. As a child I listened to stories of historical events told by my grandmother, aunts, and older cousins. When I became a practitioner of Taoism, I was immediately attracted to stories about the lives and times of the Taoist sages. My study of the history of Taoism soon went beyond the historical records into the traditions of oral and written storytelling. What I found about Taoism in these traditions far exceeded what I had expected. I was in turn surprised, delighted, amused, and even shocked.

Some of the stories went into my earlier book *Tales of the Taoist Immortals,* which explored the teachings of Taoism through the lives of its sages. In *Tales of the Dancing Dragon,* I continue the tradition of storytelling, this time to chronicle the history of Taoism and the evolution of its teachings. My sources for the stories in this book are the storytellers of Hong Kong and the chronicles known as the wild history (*yeshi*) of China. And wild it is indeed, for the writing of yeshi was never monitored by the Hanlin Academy, the imperial school of scholars and historians that wrote and compiled the "official" histories of dynastic China.

Introduction

The View of History

To understand the history of Taoism, we need to understand the Chinese view of history. First, for the Chinese, even among those who write the official histories, to achieve an "objective" or "unbiased" view of the past has never been the goal. History is meant to teach, not merely inform. Therefore, in the Chinese mind, history is always reconstructive. Even the written history of the dynasties is laced with nuances of judgment and speculations of "what could have happened." To be recorded in history is to be "judged" by history, and to study history is to learn from it.

Second, in the Chinese mind, history and philosophy are interwoven, constantly shaping each other so that neither can be understood independent of the other. Moreover, in Chinese culture the notion of "change" is pivotal to understanding the course of events. All things are subject to change, philosophical and spiritual traditions included. This is probably why the Taoist canon, the body of Taoist scriptures, is an open canon, with texts being added to it continually. Wisdom is timeless and unchanging, but attempts at understanding wisdom are not. Our glimpses of wisdom will change as human experience changes over time.

Third, in Chinese culture, history and storytelling are closely related. Even the events chronicled by the Grand Historian Sima Qian contain elements of storytelling. The storyteller has always occupied an honored position in traditional Chinese society. It is through the eyes of the storyteller that ordinary people view history, and it is through their speech that the people hear the living voice of wisdom.

The Organization of History

In telling the story of Taoism, I have organized historical events into epochs and episodes. An epoch is a historical period with a distinct theme. Each epoch has its own color and atmosphere, which is unique to that period of history. An episode, on the other hand, is a cluster of events that defines the epoch. Each episode is triggered by certain social, historical, economic, and political conditions. In turn, the occurrence of episodes opens the possibility for the emergence of other episodes and epochs.

Based on what is commonly recognized by Taoists as landmarks in the history of the spiritual tradition, I have delineated five epochs—the Legendary Times; the Qin and Han dynasties and the Three Kingdoms; the Wei, Jin, and Northern and Southern dynasties; the Sui, Tang, and Song dynasties; and the Yuan, Ming, and Qing dynasties. Each epoch has a common underlying theme, or "big picture." The Legendary Times describes the Taoist view of the creation of the cosmos and the development of early Chinese civilization. The period of the Qin and Han dynasties and the Three Kingdoms marks Taoism's entry into politics, first as a victim and later as a participant in shaping the course of history. The era of the Wei, Jin, and Northern and Southern dynasties is often called the Golden Age of Taoism—a time when major lineages of Taoism were founded. In the Sui, Tang, and Song dynasties, Taoism became a formidable force in shaping the destinies of both emperors and dynasties. Finally, in the Yuan, Ming, and Qing dynasties we witness the departure of Taoism from politics. In this era Taoism seems to have turned its energy toward strengthening its roots and nourishing its branches. The canon was compiled, and two of its major lineages—Complete Reality Taoism and the Celestial Teacher's Way—developed a network of monasteries and temples that would help Taoism survive a political and social upheaval that could have wiped out the entire spiritual tradition.

Introduction

The Legendary Times

Since there is little to no written record of the Legendary Times, the events in this period are more myth than history and more legend than chronicle.

Creation is seen as the emergence of yin and yang, female and male, from the primordial undifferentiated energy of Tao. Through the copulation of these two forces, all things in the universe were created. Civilization began when the great teachers of humanity, spirit beings who are part animal and part human, taught the ancestral peoples agriculture, animal husbandry, divination, and the healing arts. The most prominent of these teachers were Fu Xi, the father of the divination arts, and Shen Nong, the founder of Chinese herbal medicine.

The early utopian societies ended with dynastic China. The Xia dynasty, which began its rule in the twenty-third century B.C.E., was overthrown by the Shang in the eighteenth century B.C.E. The Shang in turn was conquered by King Wen of the Zhou in the twelfth century B.C.E. With the commencement of written history during the Zhou dynasty, the epoch of the Legendary Times came to an end.

The Qin and Han Dynasties, and the Period of the Three Kingdoms

The epoch of the Qin and Han dynasties and the period of the Three Kingdoms saw the emergence and development of the Taoist intellectual class—diviners, alchemists, magicians, and healers. In this period the Taoist community ventured into politics, first as experts in the arts of longevity and immortality and later as reformers and revolutionaries. In the Qin dynasty (221–207 B.C.E.), the Taoist intellectuals and the fangshi who were magicians, diviners, and herbalists found themselves entangled in an emperor's obsession with immortality. Unable to comprehend the dangers associated with a despotic government, the fangshi community was persecuted and almost exterminated.

Taoism's second venture into politics was more proactive. In fact, it was often synonymous with populist uprisings. During the latter part of the Han dynasty (206 B.C.E.–219 C.E.), especially during the Three Kingdoms Period (220 C.E.), a form of Taoism that focused on healing and exorcism attracted many followers from the lower social classes—people who had suffered most from the greed and corruption of the established government. Taoist-led movements to reform and even replace the ruling dynasty occurred throughout China toward the end of the Han. The leaders of these movements included idealistic pacifists such as Kan Zhong and Yu Qi, reformers and politicians such as Zhang Lu, and militant revolutionaries such as Zhang Jiao, the leader of the Yellow Turban rebellion.

Although the Taoist-inspired insurrections in this epoch were short-lived and its leaders often died violent deaths, the victim—Taoism—eventually ended up as the victor. The persecution of the Taoist rebels drove them underground, forcing them to spread their teachings secretly. The more oppressive the government was toward Taoism, the stronger and more widespread Taoism became. Thus when the Jin dynasty (265–420 C.E.) finally defeated its rivals and united China, Taoism was ready to exert its influence again.

The Wei, Jin, and Northern and Southern Dynasties

Some of the most turbulent times in Chinese history occurred in the epoch of the Wei, Jin and Northern and Southern dynasties. Ironically, this is also the Golden Age of Taoism. While short-lived dynasties replaced one another, Taoism flowered. Two major Taoist lineages—the Shangqing (High Purity) School and the Lingbao (Precious Luminous) School—emerged during this era, and the Celestial Teacher's Way, which had suffered decades of decline and corruption, enjoyed a major revival.

In a twist of fate, the followers of Celestial Teacher's Taoism not only saved the lives of the royal family of the Jin dynasty but also helped them consolidate power in southern China. These events were like small pebbles that started an avalanche. Taoism, especially the Celestial Teacher's Way, was transformed overnight from an underground populist movement into a mainstream religious organization.

During this epoch there was also a revival of interest in Taoist philosophy and cosmology that was spearheaded by intellectuals such as Wang Bi and the Seven Sages of the Bamboo Grove, of which Kai Kang was a member.

While Taoist intellectuals such as Kai Kang chose to disengage themselves from politics to the point of mocking the establishment, others advised kings on political and religious reforms. It was their close relationship with the ruling monarchs that allowed Lu Xiujing and Guo Qianzhi to reform and revive the Celestial Teacher's Way during the Northern and Southern dynasties. In the hands of these two Taoists, Celestial Teacher's Way was transformed from grassroots animistic magic into state religion.

Between philosophical and magical Taoism lies the mystical path of the Shangqing School and the ritualistic and Buddhist-influenced Lingbao School. The founders of these two schools— Lady Wei Huacun and Ge Xuan—were neither opponents of the establishment like Kai Kong nor active participants in court politics like Guo Qianzhi. The practitioners of the Shangqing School integrated contemplative living with practices of trance-like meditation and the visualization of deities. At the other end of the spiritual spectrum was Ge Xuan's Lingbao School, which favored group practice of rituals and the recitation of liturgy and mantras. No other epoch saw such creative innovations in Taoist thought and practices.

The Sui, Tang, and Song Dynasties

Taoists were frequent advisers if not "regular fixtures" in the Chinese imperial court during the epoch of the Sui, Tang, and Song dynasties. The founders of both the Sui (589–618 C.E.) and Tang (618–906 C.E.) dynasties sought the medicine sage Sun Xiyao for advice. While the Sui monarch rejected Xiyao's advice, the Tang emperor Taizong not only understood Xiyao's teachings that body and mind are cultivated through rigorous training and simple living but also accepted that a ruler should place his duty toward the welfare of his people before interests in attaining longevity and immortality.

During the middle of the Tang dynasty, the emperor Xuanzong had a group of close advisers that included some of the most famous Taoists of the time—Immortal Zhang Guolao, the priest Ye Fashan, and the hermit Luo Gongyuan. From the casual way these Taoists interacted with the emperor and the ease with which they moved around the imperial palace, we know that Taoism had become a part of the political establishment. Luo Gongyuan even figured significantly in helping the emperor regain his throne after an uprising had forced the royal family to flee the capital. In the Song dynasty it was Cai Fu the Incorruptible Judge, appearing as a deity, who helped Song emperor Gaozong to escape capture and revive his dynasty.

The Song dynasty also saw the rise of the Complete Reality School of Taoism and its division into a northern and a southern branch. It is said that the Song dynasty is *the* era of Southern Complete Reality Taoism because the lineage produced five great teachers—Liu Haichan, Zhang Boduan, Shi Tai, Chen Niwan, and Bai Yuchan. The teachings of these masters took Taoism to great heights when they integrated the meditation methods of the Complete Reality School founder Wang Chongyang, and the sexual alchemy (consort practice) of Lu Dongbin to form a unique approach to cultivating body and mind.

Introduction

The Yuan, Ming, and Qing Dynasties

The end of Taoism's active role in Chinese politics is marked by the Yuan, Ming, and Qing dynasties. Although Qui Changchun had advised Genghis Khan on succession, and the Longmen branch of Complete Reality Taoism was generously endowed by Kublai Khan, the Mongols were followers of Tibetan Buddhism, and Tibetan lamas replaced Taoist priests as imperial spiritual advisers. During the Ming dynasty, although Zhang Yuchu received imperial patronage in compiling the Taoist canon, his activities were scholastic, not political. European influence was also beginning to enter China, and the Ming emperors often befriended Jesuit priests to expedite the importing of firearms into China. In the Qing dynasty, even after Emperor Yongzheng was cured by Celestial Teacher priest Lou Jinhuan, members of the Taoist community never reentered court politics. In fact, by the time of the Qing, there were no more spiritual teachers serving as political advisers to monarchs.

What do we learn by studying the history of Taoism? We learn that Taoism is a dynamic spiritual tradition, changing history and at the same time being changed by history. While the essence of the teachings is timeless, the way the teachings of Taoism have manifested is not static. In the stories of Taoism, we encounter the makers of the spiritual tradition—the hermits, politicians, social activists, revolutionaries, scholars, scientists, and mystics. We participate in its defeats and victories as we plunge into the depths of its decadence and rise to the heights of its spiritual triumphs. As we travel through its birth, growth, maturation, decay, and renewal, we appreciate the richness of the lineage. The history of Taoism is indeed like the dance of the dragon, forever a display of the eternal unfolding of wisdom.

Part One

THE LEGENDARY TIMES

1

The Great Beginning

IN THE BEGINNING, if it could be called a beginning, was the primordial womb. Within the womb was the primal and undifferentiated energy tumbling and swirling in the great chaos. Sky and earth were not separate and yin and yang had not emerged. This state of timeless time and spaceless space is called Wuji, the Limitless.

Out of the Limitless emerged a being named Peng Gu. For millions of years Peng Gu lived alone, wandering in the undifferentiated chaos of the primordial womb. Then yin and yang separated. The clear and weightless vapor rose and became heaven and the muddy and heavy vapor sank and became earth. Although there were now structure and form in the cosmos, all things were still intertwined and locked in eternal embrace. This state of interconnectedness is called Taiji, the Great Limit.

Peng Gu built a home on a mountain in the center of the celestial realm. He called the mountain Seven Treasures Peak and named his abode Jade Terrace of the Mysterious City. When Peng Gu grew tired of wandering, he would return to his home on the mountain, where he would meditate in stillness and ingest the vapors of yin and yang.

Peng Gu at Jade Terrace of the Mysterious City.

Millions of years passed. Peng Gu was content to live in the celestial realm, believing that he was the only living being in the universe. But Peng Gu was not alone. Far from Peng Gu's mountain, in a remote region of the celestial realm, lived a woman named the Jade Maiden. The Jade Maiden had emerged from a spring flowing out of a cave at the same time Peng Gu was born. She too wandered in the realm of the Limitless, absorbing the essences of heaven and earth and swallowing the light of the sun and the moon.

One day in his travels, Peng Gu caught a glimpse of the Jade Maiden as she floated among the azure clouds. Taken by her beauty, he immediately invited her to live with him on Seven Treasures Mountain. There in his golden bedchamber, he entered her and she received him, he absorbing her generative blood and she accepting his life force. Out of their union emerged the Emperor of the East and the Empress of the West. The Emperor of the East is the manifestation of the energy and essence of the Great Yang, and the Empress of the West is the manifestation of the energy and essence of the Great Yin. They are also known respectively as Father Wood and Mother Metal.

Peng Gu and the Jade Maiden also gave birth to the Celestial Lord. The Celestial Lord gave birth to the Terrestrial Lord, and the Terrestrial Lord in turn gave birth to the Lord of Humanity. From these lords were born the myriad deities, the immortals, and the teachers of humanity.

2

Fu Xi and the Precelestial *Bagua*

AFTER HEAVEN AND EARTH separated, yin and yang copulated. From this copulation countless myriad things emerged. Because these entities differed in the manner they partook of the essences of yin and yang, they became different in kind and nature. Those that contained more of the essence of stillness became trees, grasses, and roots; those that contained more of the essence of movement became birds, mammals, fishes, and insects; and those that contained more of the essence of spirit became humans. It is also said that of all sentient beings, humans alone embrace equally the essence of heaven and the splendors of earth; therefore they have the gift to understand the subtle mysteries of creation.

In ancient times people lived simply. They drank sweet dew from the leaves and inhaled mist from the mountains and lakes. They knew nothing about happiness and sorrow and gain and loss. Their lives revolved around the cycle of the seasons and the paths of the sun, moon, and stars. Following the natural way, they lived long and contented lives.

Thousands of years passed. The Early Ancient Era passed into the Middle Ancient Era, which in turn passed into the Later Ancient Era. In the Later Ancient Era there lived a sage named Fu Xi. Legends say that Fu Xi had a man's head and a snake's body. He taught the people hunting, fishing, animal husbandry, and writing.

When Fu Xi saw that the people could provide for themselves, he turned his attention to understanding the nature of the universe. First he studied the paths of the sun, moon, and stars. Then he examined the patterns of the mountains, lakes, and rivers. Finally he pondered the nature of the wind, rain, and thunder. From these observations, Fu Xi concluded that there are eight fundamental building blocks of the natural world—sky, earth, water, fire, thunder, wind, mountain, and lake. Furthermore, these eight can be characterized by the way they embody and manifest the principles of yin and yang. He named them the *bagua,* or the eight trigrams.

Sky embodies the pure essence of the clear brightness of yang; therefore its trigram is depicted as three solid, or yang, lines (☰). Earth embodies the pure essence of the dark mysteries of earth; therefore its trigram is depicted as three broken, or yin, lines (☷). Water is externally soft and yielding, but within its softness is a strength that can break down mountains; thus its trigram is depicted as two yin lines flanking a yang line (☵). Fire is strong externally, but within its strength is the softness of warmth; thus its trigram is depicted as two yang lines flanking a yin line (☲). Thunder is associated with spring rain and the first stirring of life after winter; therefore its trigram is depicted as a yang line at the bottom, symbolizing the return of life, with two yin lines on top, symbolizing the nourishing nature of spring showers (☳). Just as thunder is associated with the renewal of life, wind is associated with the coming of winter. The trigram of wind is depicted as two yang lines on top of a yin line, symbolizing cold winds undermining the last warmth before winter (☴). Mountains are associated with hardness because they appear jagged and rocky. However, their roots anchor deep into the earth. The trigram of mountain is therefore depicted as a yang line on top, symbolizing the rocky peaks thrusting up to the sky, with two yin lines at the bottom, symbolizing the mountain's roots penetrating into the earth (☶). Finally, a lake is a body of water whose surface is soft and pliable, but within its depth is a strength that can support myriad life forms. Thus the trigram of lake is depicted as a yin line on top of two yang lines (☱).

Because the eight trigrams are said to describe the way things exist naturally before the intervention of humankind, they are known as the precelestial (or precreation) bagua.

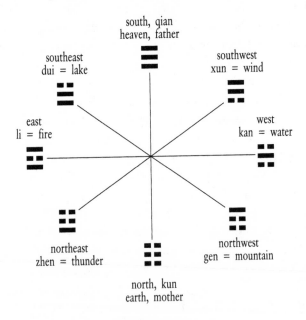

The pre-celestial bagua.

3

Shen Nong the Herbalist

LEGEND HAS IT that Shen Nong was conceived when his mother swallowed the vapor of a celestial dragon. Nine days after conception, Shen Nong's mother gave birth by the river Jiang. The infant that tumbled out of the womb had a bull's head and a man's body. Three days after emerging from his mother's womb, Shen Nong was able to speak. Five days later he could walk, and seven days later his teeth were fully formed. When Shen Nong grew to manhood, he towered more than eight feet.

Shen Nong had a natural affinity for plants. Even as a child he was fascinated by the healing properties of herbs and fungi. When Shen Nong heard that there was a man who knew the secrets of the healing powers of plants, he decided to go and learn from him. However, when the hopeful student arrived at the herbalist's hut, he was met by a young apprentice who told him, "My master has gone into the mountains to gather herbs."

"When will your teacher return?" asked Shen Nong.

The boy replied, "He could be gone for a week, a month, or a year. Who knows?"

Determined to learn from the herb master, Shen Nong said, "I will build a hut nearby and wait for the teacher to return."

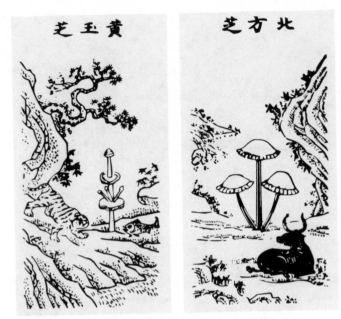

Magical fungi—illustration from "Book of Herb Lore," Taoist Canon.

Seeing Shen Nong's sincerity, the boy said, "Perhaps I can help you. What is it that you wish to learn?"

Shen Nong said, "I'm puzzled by the fact that in ancient times people lived long and healthy lives but nowadays they get sick easily and often die before their time."

The boy replied, "In ancient times people knew how to take care of themselves. They rose at sunrise and rested at sunset. Never exerting themselves, they lived simply and had few desires. Knowing that it was better to prevent illnesses than to try to cure them, they ate healthy foods and did not expose themselves to excessive heat or cold. And when they got sick, they knew how to apply the appropriate remedies. Today people hardly pay attention to their health: they don't eat properly, they don't rest sufficiently, and they squander their life energy by indulging in excessive sexual activity. Worse, when they fall ill, they don't know the correct treatment. Consequently, illnesses that can be cured easily often end up being serious or fatal."

Shen Nong asked, "How can I help people to live a healthy and long life?"

The boy said, "You'll need to study the medicinal qualities of plants." He handed Shen Nong a bamboo scroll and continued, "Use this as a guide. However, if you really want to understand the healing nature of plants, you'll have to experiment with them."

Shen Nong took the book and bowed. When he looked up, the boy and the hut had disappeared.

Shen Nong returned home. He studied the book of herbs, and following the advice of the master herbalist, he traveled throughout the land, identifying, learning, and cataloging medicinal herbs and fungi. Shen Nong eventually cataloged 365 medicinal plants and wrote lengthy descriptions of their healing properties and method of infusion.

Shen Nong also taught the people how to farm crops for food and weave plant fibers into cloth. Most important, he taught them the need to protect plant habitats, for if the places where the plants grow were destroyed, the science of herbal medicine would be lost to humanity forever.

4

King Wen's Hexagrams

THE LAST EMPEROR of the Shang dynasty, Zou, was a tyrant who cared only for luxuries and beautiful women. Ministers who advised him to attend to the affairs of the kingdom were usually tortured or killed. The gruesome executions were often supervised by the mad emperor himself, who laughed as he watched the victims being lowered into burning oil or crushed beneath stampeding horses.

The ordinary citizen did not escape the king's madness either. Farmers were conscripted to build extravagant palaces, and merchants were forced to supply goods without compensation. The economy was in shambles; corrupt ministers filled their coffers while peasants starved, flood and famine plagued the nation, and bandits roamed the countryside robbing villages and trade caravans.

In the west, far from the capital, lay the feudal kingdom of Zhou, whose rulers were vassals of the Shang emperor. The leader of the Zhou clan, Ji Chang, was a man of honor and virtue. Seeing the state his country had degenerated into, he decided to plead before the emperor on behalf of the people. When Ji Chang arrived at the capital, he was immediately arrested. Afraid that Ji Chang would accuse them of corruption and incompetence, the emperor's advisers informed Zou that the vassal lord was planning a rebellion.

That Ji Chang was the lord of a prosperous and powerful vassal kingdom probably saved his life. The emperor was afraid that if the Zhou lord were killed, his sons might take revenge. So he had Ji Chang detained in the capital as a hostage.

Ji Chang's prison was a one-room cottage with a small courtyard. He was given the basic necessities of food and a bed but was not allowed books or visitors. Unable to communicate with his family, Chang accepted his fate and passed the days thinking and the nights observing the stars. It was during his imprisonment that Ji Chang began to ponder the meaning of Fu Xi's bagua. Fu Xi's bagua described a time when everything existed in harmonious balance. In Ji Chang's own time, things were anything but balanced and harmonious. The country had an emperor who delighted in killing, an administration that was corrupt, and a people that was suffering under heavy taxation and forced labor. Ji Chang began to question whether Fu Xi's bagua could describe the imbalanced and insane world he lived in. After much thought, Ji Chang expanded Fu Xi's bagua so that it could be applied to the conditions of his time. Ji Chang took each trigram, paired it with each of the other eight, and created sixty-four hexagrams, or patterns of six lines.

Ji Chang also came to the conclusion that to understand the way things are, he needed to know how they came to be as well as how they would change in the future. Drawing on his knowledge of the nature of change (*yi*), Ji Chang devised a system of divination based on the sixty-four hexagrams.

In Ji Chang's system of divination, each hexagram carried a message. The key to casting the divination lay in how a hexagram is selected to reveal the message. After much pondering, Ji Chang came up with the following method of obtaining the hexagram: First he took a branch and broke it into six equal sections. Next, using the jade from his belt buckle, he etched a

坤 地	艮 山	坎 水	巽 風	震 雷	離 火	兌 澤	乾 天	上卦／下卦
地天泰	山天大畜	水天需	風天小畜	雷天大壯	火天大有	澤天夬	乾為天	天
地澤臨	山澤損	水澤節	風澤中孚	雷澤歸妹	火澤睽	兌為澤	天澤履	澤
地火明夷	山火賁	水火既濟	風火家人	雷火豐	離為火	澤火革	天火同人	火
地雷復	山雷頤	水雷屯	風雷益	震為雷	火雷噬嗑	澤雷隨	天雷无妄	雷
地風升	山風蠱	水風井	巽為風	雷風恒	火風鼎	澤風大過	天風姤	風
地水師	山水蒙	坎為水	風水渙	雷水解	火水未濟	澤水困	天水訟	水
地山謙	艮為山	水山蹇	風山漸	雷山小過	火山旅	澤山咸	天山遯	山
坤為地	山地剝	水地比	風地觀	雷地豫	火地晉	澤地萃	天地否	地

The sixty-four hexagrams.

broken line on each of three twigs and a solid line on the rest. Then he placed the twigs in a cloth bag. Focusing his mind on the subject he wanted to divine, he drew three sticks from the bag to determine the first line of the hexagram. If the majority of the sticks he had drawn had broken lines, that line of the hexagram would be yin. If the majority of the sticks had solid lines, that line would be yang. Repeating the procedure five times, Ji Chang got his hexagram.

One day, after having been imprisoned for almost six years, Ji Chang decided to divine whether he had a chance of returning home. The hexagram that emerged from the divination was "Xie" or "Release," indicating that his release was imminent but at a high price.

Back in the kingdom of Zhou, Ji Chang's sons were discussing how they could free their father.

Ji Chang's eldest son volunteered to take his father's place as hostage.

The second son, Ji Fa, argued that the plan was too risky. "You're assuming that the emperor is reasonable. What if this madman detains both you and Father? Then we'll lose both our lord and his successor."

There was a long silence. Then Ji Fa turned to the youngest brother and said, "You're the most learned among us and have always had good intuition. What do you suggest?"

The youngest son of Ji Chang replied, "If our eldest brother goes to the capital, we'll lose him, but our father will be saved. If no one goes, we'll lose our father, but our brother will live. Which life should we save and which should we lose? One is my father's; the other is my brother's. How can I choose between them?"

The eldest son said, "If I can save my father by forfeiting my life, then the matter is closed. I will go and exchange places with him."

The other brothers each volunteered themselves, but the eldest said, "Of the three of us, I am the most expendable. I'm not a military genius like Ji Fa nor a scholar and a talented administrator like our youngest brother. Zhou will need a general to defeat the Shang, and after defeating the Shang, our dynasty will need a good minister to run it. I'm the one who should go. If by my death our father can return to lead our clan to our destiny, my life will have been well lived."

Ji Chang's eldest son journeyed to the capital and sought an audience with the emperor. Bowing before his lord, he said, "My father is getting old and is not in good health. Please allow me to take his place so that he can return home."

Emperor Zou laughed at the request and said sarcastically, "What a filial son! Let's see if your father appreciates your filial duty." The emperor ordered Ji Chang's son killed and his body cut into pieces and cooked.

Chuckling, he said, "I want to watch the old man eat his son's flesh and bones."

The platter of his son's remains was brought before Ji Chang. "I have prepared a sumptuous dinner for you," the emperor said. "It is your eldest son's flesh and blood."

The meat was forced into Ji Chang's mouth. Ji Chang wanted to spit it out, but something made him change his mind. He remembered the divination and realized that his son's death was the price of his escape. Silently he thanked his eldest son for his sacrifice and swallowed the meat.

"So, was the meat cooked to your liking?" Zou asked viciously.

Ji Chang replied, "Yes, lord, it was tasty."

"You do *know* that it was your son's flesh, don't you?" taunted the emperor.

Ji Chang mumbled, "As long as it tasted good, it doesn't matter whose son it is."

Hearing this, the emperor thought, "This man is so senile that he doesn't know what he's talking about. No sane man would enjoy eating the flesh of his own son. He's no longer useful to me as a hostage. What's more, killing an insane man is not as entertaining as killing a man with a clear mind." Turning to the guards he said, "Throw him out and let him die as a beggar in the streets."

Once Ji Chang was free, he quickly made his way back to his kingdom. When the two sons saw their father, they knew that their eldest brother was dead. Ji Chang had expected the price of his escape to be high, but it was not until he was forced to eat his son's flesh that he realized that his "release" depended on how skillfully he handled the situation. The divination did not reveal to him his son's death, but if Ji Chang had not divined, he would not have responded in a way that would make the tyrant believe he was a useless hostage.

Immediately after his return to Zhou, Ji Chang took counsel with his sons and ministers and prepared for the conquest of the Shang. In the spring of 1122 B.C.E., the old patriarch and his sons rode out from their capital: they had a war to fight and a family member to avenge. Dressed in white robes of mourning, Ji Chang and his army marched toward the Shang capital. Inside his palace, emperor Zou slaughtered his wives and children and then committed suicide. The Shang dynasty capitulated and was replaced by the Zhou. Ji Chang was crowned as King Wen, the scholar-emperor. The system of divination he had devised in prison, called King Wen's Method, is still used widely among Chinese diviners today.

Ji Fa, the general of the victorious Zhou army, succeeded his father and was named Zhou Wuwang, the martial emperor. Ji Chang's youngest son, Zhou Gong, served his father and brother as prime minister and established an administration that brought peace and prosperity to China for four hundred years.

5

Peng Zu and
Emperor Zhou Mu

LEGEND TELLS US that Peng Zu was the first person to attain longevity and immortality. During the Shang dynasty, Peng Zu was already seven hundred years old. When the Zhou replaced the Shang, the Zhou emperor Mu visited Peng Zu and asked the sage to serve as minister. Peng Zu declined.

Not long afterward, Emperor Mu asked Peng Zu to teach him the arts of longevity. Peng Zu refused. When the emperor tried to entice the sage with gifts of gold and jewels, the sage took the gifts and distributed them to the poor. No matter how the emperor begged, cajoled, and threatened, Peng Zu would not say a word.

One day a beautiful woman by the name of Cui visited Peng Zu in his mountain cottage. Peng knew that the woman had been sent by the emperor to pry the secrets of the art of longevity out of him.

Before the woman could even introduce herself, Peng Zu said, "All my life I've been a hermit. I have no interest in politics, fame, and wealth. I'm just a simple man who delights in living

Peng Zu.

a life of contentment. I have nothing to teach. If you're interested in learning the arts of longevity, you should seek Master Qingjing."

Lady Cui asked, "Is Master Qingjing an immortal?"

Peng Zu replied, "Master Qingjing is not an immortal. Rather, he's someone who has attained the Tao."

Lady Cui asked again, "What is a man of the Tao?"

Peng Zu said, "A man of the Tao lives among the people. The only difference between him and the common person is that he enjoys good health and peace of mind. His body is healthy because he knows how to cultivate the breath of life; his mind is clear because he is free from anxiety and worry. To attain longevity, you must cultivate the vital breath, and to cultivate the vital breath, you must preserve procreative energy. Know your limits. Do not indulge in excessive sexual activity. Lock the generative energy within, swallow the vapors of the sun and the moon, massage yourself, and ingest herbs and fungi to moisten your skin and nourish your internal organs. Follow these instructions and you'll attain longevity."

Lady Cui bowed and left. Returning to Emperor Mu, she related to him everything she had learned from Peng Zu. The emperor tried to practice the techniques described by the sage, but lacking discipline and proper instruction, he was able to experience only small benefits. Angry and frustrated, the king summoned his personal guards and said, "Bring Peng Zu and Qingjing to my palace, by force if necessary."

When the guards arrived at Peng Zu's cottage, the sage could not be found. When they enquired about the mysterious Master Qingjing, it appeared that no one had ever seen or heard of him.

Part Two

The Qin and Han Dynasties, and the Period of the Three Kingdoms

6

Xu Fu's Voyage to the Islands of Immortality

AFTER CENTURIES OF civil war, China was united under the Qin dynasty in 221 B.C.E. The first emperor of Qin instituted sweeping economic and social reforms by standardizing currency, measurements, and written language. Roads were improved, canals were dug to facilitate river trade, and patrols were sent to guard caravan routes. The emperor even began the great project of constructing an earthen wall to protect the frontier. However, despite the economic boom, two things still haunted the Qin emperor: uprisings and his own death.

To prevent the outbreak of rebellion, the emperor outlawed the discussion of politics and planted spies to monitor the activities of the intellectual community. Those who dared criticize the government were imprisoned or executed for treason. The emperor also kept a close watch on the healers and alchemists who were making pills and elixirs of immortality from herbs, fungi, and minerals. As the emperor aged, his obsession with searching for ways to attain immortality increased.

One time the emperor was informed that in a village along the eastern coast there lived a man who never aged. When asked how he had attained longevity, the man claimed that he had ingested herbs that he had found on islands across the sea. The emperor immediately sent an emissary to the coastal village to learn the whereabouts of the islands. However, when the imperial messenger arrived, he was told that the strange man had sailed off and disappeared.

The emperor was outraged and had both the informer and the messenger executed for incompetence. Frustrated and angry, he paced around listlessly. A minister, noticing the king's restlessness, advised him, "Your Majesty, if we offer a large reward, I'm sure someone will be able to find the herbs of immortality."

The emperor immediately issued a proclamation, offering gold, land, and title to those who could find the islands of immortality and bring back the magical herbs. Enticed by the rewards, many sailed to look for the islands, but none returned.

In a small town by the sea there lived a man named Xu Fu. Xu Fu was a fangshi, an adept in the arts of divination, herbal medicine, and sorcery. He went before the emperor and announced boldly, "I know how to find the islands of immortality in the eastern seas."

The emperor was skeptical. Sarcastically, he said, "What makes you think you will succeed when hundreds of others have failed?"

Xu Fu replied, "Your Majesty, I have lived by the sea all my life and am familiar with the winds and the currents. I am confident that I will be able to find those mysterious islands."

Xu Fu then laid out a map showing a group of islands off the eastern coast. "This map was given to me by an immortal," he said. "One day as I was gathering medicinal seaweeds along the shore, a fog blew in. A strange man emerged out of the fog and walked toward me. He handed me a scroll and instructed me to present it to the most honored person in the land."

The emperor was suddenly attentive. Xu Fu continued, "I unrolled the scroll and found that it was a map. When I looked up, the fog was gone and the strange being had disappeared." He pointed to a group of islands on the far side of the eastern sea and said, "I believe these are the islands of immortality."

"I hereby authorize you to lead an expedition to find these islands," the emperor said to Xu Fu. "You will leave immediately."

Xu Fu bowed and replied, "Your Majesty, I am honored by your trust. However, the eastern sea is stormy, and the currents around the islands are treacherous. For the mission to succeed, I will need large boats and skilled sailors to navigate the waters. And to harvest the herbs, I'll need able-bodied workers."

The emperor ordered a fleet built to carry three thousand workers. The ships were to be stocked with provisions for a year and manned by the best mariners in the country; they would sail with the spring tides.

The night before the boats departed, Xu Fu called his family and friends together and said, "I volunteered to lead the expedition to the islands of immortality not because I believed that I could find them but because of what I saw in the heavens. A year ago I saw a fireball streak across the sky and plunge into the sea. This omen forebodes the destruction of the fangshi community. Our schools will be closed, our books burned, and we will be hunted and killed. What's more, I have a premonition that war will soon be upon us. The expedition is a ruse. If we don't leave now, we may not be able to escape the impending disaster."

Xu Fu's friends were shocked. Some argued, "Why do we need to fear persecution? We've never criticized the government."

"Compared with the dangers of unknown oceans, we're much safer here," others added.

In the end only a small number of Xu Fu's relatives and friends packed their belongings and boarded the boats.

The next morning, amid fanfare and cheers, the fleet left the harbor.

The summer went by. Autumn passed, and then winter.

Xu Fu riding on the giant fish that led him to the islands of Japan.

Spring arrived, and it had been a year since Xu Fu's expedition had sailed. The emperor became impatient. He had towers built along the eastern coast and ordered guards to watch the horizon day and night. However, no boat returned that spring.

One day an herbalist appeared at the Qin court claiming that he had found the herb of immortality. The emperor summoned the man immediately and said, "Let me see the herb you have found."

The man took a strange-looking mushroom out of his bag and said, "This is the lingshi mushroom. Eat it and you will attain immortality."

The emperor was about to eat the mushroom but suddenly thought, "There have been many attempts on my life recently. What if this is a plot to poison me?" Aloud he said to the herbalist, "I will eat this plant after you have tasted it."

The herbalist swallowed the fungus. Immediately the man started to shimmer before the emperor's eyes. Before the guards could restrain him, the herbalist had dissolved into a trail of smoke.

The emperor was beside himself. He had all the fangshi rounded up and imprisoned. When no one could tell him where the mushroom of immortality could be found, he began to execute them one by one. The persecution of the fangshi drew angry whispers from the intellectual community. When the emperor learned of their criticisms, he had the intellectuals imprisoned and tortured and their libraries burned.

Desperate to attain immortality, he began to ingest mercury, lead, and sulfur, hoping that these "magical" minerals would give him eternal life. Not long afterward, the emperor died of lead and mercuric poisoning. After his death the political and economic structure that he had built broke down. A peasant rebellion toppled the government, and the Qin dynasty, which the emperor had hoped would last a millennium, ended after fifteen years.

Legends say that when Xu Fu's fleet reached the open sea, a giant fish appeared and guided the ships eastward. Xu Fu made landfall in the islands now known as Japan. He and the members of the expedition settled there and never returned to China.

7

The Three Brothers
of Mount Mao

TOWARD THE END of the Zhou dynasty, in the city of Hanyang, there lived a provincial minister by the name of Mao Meng. By that time the Zhou had gotten as corrupt and decadent as the Shang it had replaced a thousand years earlier. Mao Meng realized that sooner or later the mandate of rule would be taken away from the Zhou emperors. He therefore begged to be released from the civil service, citing reasons of ill health.

When Mao Meng heard that an adept in the Taoist arts of longevity and immortality named Master of Ghost Valley was living on Mount Hua, he left his home and journeyed to the mountain. Meng climbed the precipitous cliffs, found the master, and joined the community of students studying under him. Eventually Mao Meng attained immortality and floated away on a bed of clouds.

Seventy years later, when the Han dynasty had replaced both the Zhou and the Qin, a son was born into the family of Mao. When the child emerged from his mother's womb, a rainbow appeared and hovered over the family's home for three days. The parents were delighted, for this auspicious omen could only mean that their child would grow up to be an unusual man. They named the boy Mao Xing, meaning "one whose deeds will last for posterity."

Mao Xing began to exhibit extraordinary abilities even as a child. It was said that by six he had memorized all the Taoist and Confucian classics. By ten he was collecting herbs and practicing the arts of longevity. Initially his parents were proud of their son's abilities, but when Mao Xing showed no interest in politics or the military, they became disappointed. Father and son often argued, and Mao Xing began to spend more and more time in the mountains searching for minerals and herbs to concoct the pill of immortality.

One time, after Mao Xing had been away in the mountains for a month, his father said to him, "You are now eighteen years old and have accomplished nothing. It's about time you decide what to do with your life."

Mao Xing replied, "I want to spend the rest of my life studying and practicing the healing arts."

His father exclaimed, "What! Are you going to shame the family by becoming a wandering herbalist!"

Mao Xing said, "There is nothing shameful about finding cures for diseases and helping people to live happier and healthier lives."

His father said angrily, "If you are set in your ways, then leave us and never return."

Mao Xing took his herb basket and digging trowels and left Hanyang. He first journeyed north to Mount Heng, where he met a Taoist hermit who taught him how to regulate the breath and circulate internal energy. Then he traveled east to the mountains in Jiangsu Province, where he lived for thirty years, collecting medicinal herbs and minerals. While not in the field or in his laboratory, Mao Xing would visit the towns and villages to heal the sick and the dying.

When Mao Xing was forty-eight years old, he felt an urge to

return home to see his aging parents. However, as he entered the courtyard, he saw his father storming out, waving a stick and screaming, "You are no longer my son! How dare you step into my household!"

The father raised the stick and was about to strike Mao Xing when the son said, "Father, please hold your hand. I know I have neglected my filial duties, but I am now an immortal. The lords of heaven will be angry at you for striking someone who has attained the Tao."

His father ignored Mao Xing's plea. Just before the stick struck Xing, it disintegrated. Mao Xing's father now understood and stood trembling in fear. He stammered, "If you are an immortal, can you return someone from the dead?"

"I will do what I can," replied Mao Xing.

His father led Mao Xing to the home of a friend whose child had died recently. The two arrived just as the casket was being sealed.

Mao Xing opened the casket, took the child's hand, and said, "This child died before his time. He should be given back his life."

The child sat up immediately. Word got out that an immortal was in the village, and hundreds of the sick and injured were brought to Mao Xing for healing. To those who could be cured by herbs, Xing dispensed herbal medicine. To those with incurable diseases he gave pills that he had specially prepared in his laboratory. Everyone brought to Mao Xing was healed.

Mao Xing was forgiven by his father and welcomed back into the family.

One time Mao Xing returned home to find his father gravely ill. The old man called his eldest son to his side and said, "I have not been a wise father. A wiser man would have been a better example to his sons." After a pause, he whispered weakly, "Your brothers are foolish and stubborn. Promise me that you will guide them to the Tao." Mao Xing nodded, and his father breathed his last.

Mao Xing's brothers were officers in the provincial army. One was named Mao Gu and the other Mao Zhong. Rude and arrogant, the brothers flaunted their wealth and power wherever they went. They paraded around the streets in expensive silk robes, rode in carriages pulled by pedigreed horses, and forced townspeople to line the streets to welcome them when they inspected a city's garrison.

One time the brothers were stopped by Mao Xing as they were about to enter their favorite brothel.

"Are you going to tell us to give up our vices?" Mao Gu asked in a mocking voice. "If you are, then you're wasting your time."

Mao Xing simply said, "Next year on the third day of the fourth month, I will be leaving for the immortal realm. I hope the two of you can go to Mount Tai to see me off."

Mao Xing walked away. The two brothers looked at each other, puzzled. Mao Zhong asked Mao Gu, "What is our brother up to? Mount Tai is hundreds of miles away. Is he playing a joke on us?"

Mao Gu thought for a while and said, "I've never known our eldest brother to say anything trivial. I think we should go to Mount Tai. I have a feeling that we'll never see him again if we don't go. After all, he is our brother."

On the appointed day, the three brothers met on top of Mount Tai.

Mao Xing said to Mao Gu and Mao Zhong, "I will be leaving soon. Before I go, I have a few words of advice for you. Material wealth and pleasures of the body are impermanent. However, the Tao within you lasts forever. Think this over. When you've decided what you want to do for the rest of your lives, look for me in the mountains in the east."

Suddenly the top of Mount Tai was bathed in golden light.

Mao Xing (on cloud) bids farewell to his brothers Mao Gu and Mao Zhong.

Immortal beings floated down on purple and azure clouds. Mao Xing stepped onto the clouds and disappeared. Mao Gu and Mao Zhong understood their brother's advice at once.

The two brothers returned home and resigned their commissions in the army. Carrying meager belongings, they traveled to the mountains in the east. Gone were the silks and carriages and fine horses. In hemp robes and straw sandals, Mao Gu and Mao Zhong walked a thousand miles to search for Ma Xing.

Years later, on the forested slopes of Mount Gu in Jiangsu province, Mao Gu and Mao Zhong found Mao Xing. The three brothers built a retreat deep in the mountain, and Xing taught Gu and Zhong how to identify and collect rare medicinal herbs. Year after year the brothers climbed mountains, waded through swamps, and penetrated thick forests to gather herbs and minerals. When not in the field or their laboratory, they would visit towns and villages, dispensing medicine and healing the sick.

For fifty years the three brothers offered their healing skills and medicines freely to the people of Jiangsu Province. When they departed for the immortal realm, the people of that region honored them by renaming Mount Gu Mount Mao. Today shrines dedicated to Mao Xing, Mao Gu, and Mao Zhong are found throughout the mountain where they once lived.

8

The Huang Lao Teachings

AFTER LESS THAN twenty years of rule, the Qin dynasty fell and was replaced by the Han. Having learned the lesson that harsh laws might not be the key to building a peaceful and harmonious society, the early Han emperors minimized government bureaucracy, emphasized public works, and encouraged its nobility and citizens to live simple lives.

The government's policies were welcomed by a nation that had seen more than a thousand years of warfare and social disorder. For once, both rulers and ruled saw eye to eye: neither the feudal system of the Zhou nor the police state of the Qin was able to create a harmonious society. Tired of an unwieldy bureaucracy associated with Confucianism and leery of the dictatorship of a despot, both the emperor and the people turned to Laozi's teachings of embracing simplicity and following the natural way.

A new class of intellectuals emerged. These thinkers integrated the Taoist teachings of simplicity and nonaction with the popular belief in immortals and named this new philosophy the Huang Lao Teachings. "Huang" refers to Huangdi, the Yellow Emperor, and "Lao" refers to Laozi. The philosophical basis of the Huang Lao Teachings was Laozi's *Daode Jing*, and the first avatar of this spiritual movement was the Yellow Emperor, generally believed by many to be the first mortal to attain immortality.

So popular was the Huang Lao philosophy that Taoist teachers were often guests at the court of the Han emperor Wen. In one of his meetings with the Huang Lao philosophers, the emperor was informed that far to the west lived a sage of great wisdom. Eager to meet this enlightened being, the emperor immediately sent a messenger to summon the Taoist to the capital. However, when the emissary met the sage he was told, "The Tao cannot be summoned and dismissed at will."

Hearing this, Emperor Wen realized his mistake. He humbled himself and traveled to the western frontier. Accompanied by a retinue of ministers and guards, the emperor arrived at the sage's hut. A pavilion was erected, and the emperor sat and waited for the sage to greet him. After a while, an old man appeared and stood before the emperor. The king was not pleased that the Taoist did not prostrate or even bow before him. In an authoritative voice, Emperor Wen said, "I am the lord of this land and nation. I own the very ground you are standing upon. You may be a sage, but you're still a citizen of my country. When you see your emperor, you should kneel and pay your respect. I have the power to make you rich or poor."

The sage said nothing. Then, slowly, in front of the emperor, he floated up to the treetops and said calmly, "I no longer stand on the earth you 'own.' Why should I bow before you?"

The emperor was startled. He immediately went on his knees and said, "I did not know you are an immortal. Please forgive my disrespect."

The sage replied, "I am no immortal. I don't even know what immortality means. I'm just a simple man who has decided to return after having lived in the west."

Emperor Wen realized that the man floating in front of him

*Laozi on clouds. Typical image of Laozi dating
from the Han dynasty.*

was Laozi. He therefore bowed and said, "Most honored one, please instruct me on how to bring peace and harmony to my country."

Laozi replied, "Follow the path of nonaction, and do not interfere with the natural way of things. Nourish the land and the people, but do not own them. When your subjects no longer know what it means to be ruled and not ruled, there will be peace and harmony."

The sage disappeared, leaving behind a rainbow hovering over the tree. Emperor Wen returned to the capital and took the words of Laozi to heart. He followed the Huang Lao Teachings and lived a simple life. Because the emperor and his court did not indulge in extravagances, the government was able to lower taxes, institute agricultural reforms, and take preventive measures against floods and famine. Emperor Wen's son, Jing, continued the policies of his father. By the end of the reign of these two emperors, the nation enjoyed a peace and prosperity that rivaled the early years of the Zhou dynasty.

The reigns of these two Han emperors were described by historians as "the enlightened and glorious rule of Wen and Jing."

9

The Way of Harmony and Peace

IN THE LATTER PART of the Han dynasty, the imperial court was decadent and the ministers corrupt. As one inept emperor succeeded another, eunuchs emerged as the power behind the throne. Public works were neglected, frontier garrisons were understaffed, and taxes were levied to support the extravagances of the royal family.

In these troubled times there lived a Taoist named Kan Zhong who was not only an adept in the arts of health and longevity but also an expert in statecraft, military strategy, and diplomacy. Among Zhong's many students were sons of ministers and generals. Thus, although Kan Zhong did not hold a position in the government, he had plenty of eyes and ears in the capital.

The decadence of the Han court affected Kan Zhong deeply. While most of his Taoist friends stayed out of politics, Zhong believed that given the right guidance, the government could be reformed and its mandate of rule be renewed. Integrating the Huang Lao Teachings of noninterference with the Confucian principle of propagating harmony between heaven, earth, and humanity, Kan Zhong developed a philosophy that he named

Kan Zhong.

the Taiping Way, meaning the Way of Harmony and Peace. The Taiping Way instructed monarchs to follow the will of heaven, encouraged people to practice the arts of health and longevity, and taught that promoting peace and harmony should be the goal of every nation.

Kan Zhong's students spread the ideals of the Way of Harmony and Peace throughout the cities and countryside, proclaiming that their mentor had received the teachings directly from the immortals.

In less troubled times, Kan Zhong's teachings would have been welcomed and appreciated by the government. But in a time when the Han court was plagued with conspiracies, and with many of Zhong's students being members of the aristocracy, the teachings of the Taiping Way were deemed too dangerous to be tolerated. After a student of Kan Zhong's got entangled in a failed plot to remove some powerful eunuchs from the emperor's side, Kan Zhong was arrested and executed for treason. His students went into hiding but continued to spread the teachings secretly in the northern provinces, where the Han empire's influence was at best weak. From the north, the influence of the Taiping Way gradually entered central and southeastern China.

At this time the Han empire was divided into numerous semi-autonomous states, with the kingdom of Wu being the most enterprising and aggressive. In Wu there lived a Taoist healer and diviner named Yu Qi. Yu Qi had been weak and sickly as a child but was cured by a wandering healer. Admiring his benefactor's skills, Qi gave up a comfortable life to follow the mysterious man into the mountains. Years later Yu Qi returned to his native town with skills of divination, talismanic magic, and herbal medicine. He also had a scroll given to him by his teacher. This scroll was a copy of *The Book of Harmony and Peace*, and in it were the teachings of Kan Zhong.

Yu Qi was amazed at what was taught in *The Book of Harmony and Peace*. The text covered topics ranging from the arts of health and longevity to divination, statecraft, and military strategy. It described the three components of internal energy—generative, vital, and spirit—and the methods to cultivate them: spirit energy is cultivated by stilling the mind, generative energy by minimizing sexual activity, and vital energy by controlling and regulating the breath. It classified and described six levels of enlightenment: the deified being (the highest), followed by the realized being, the immortal, the Taoist adept, the sage, and the virtuous person. It asserted that those aspiring to become deities, realized beings, and immortals must still the mind, keep the true spirit within, hold on to the oneness of the Tao, and cultivate and purify the three internal energies.

Yu Qi wandered throughout the state of Wu, teaching the philosophy of Kan Zhong and healing the sick. If *The Book of Harmony and Peace* were concerned only with cultivating health, longevity, and immortality, Yu Qi would not have offended the rulers of Wu. However, the book advocated the creation of a utopian state whose kings followed the will of heaven, honored the earth, and attended to the needs of humanity. In a political climate where feudal lords were disrespectful of the weak emperor and eagerly planning to decimate their rivals, such ideas were not tolerated.

Yu Qi's reputation as a sage and healer grew like wildfire in Wu. Even the dowager of Wu became one of his devoted followers. One time Yu Qi happened to be in the company of the matriarch when the lord of Wu visited his mother. The dowager called her son to her side and said, "Come and listen to the advice of a wise man."

The lord of Wu, Sun Ce, was skeptical of everything spiritual and considered Taoism no more than a mumbo jumbo of words. As far as he was concerned, Yu Qi was a charlatan who should not be meddling in the politics of Wu.

However, Sun Ce did not want to offend his mother, so he sat down quietly.

Yu Qi bowed to Ce and said, "My lord, if you respect peace, your people will prosper. The way of peace is the way of heaven. If you go against the way of heaven, you will meet a violent death."

The lord of Wu was planning to invade a neighboring state. When he heard Yu Qi's words, he was not pleased.

"Since when have the lords of Wu listened to charlatans?" Sun Ce said to himself. "This man is stirring up trouble and must be eliminated."

The next day the lord of Wu had Yu Qi arrested and brought before him.

"You claim to possess magical powers," Sun Ce said to Yu Qi. "If you can save yourself, I'll listen to your advice. If not, you've proved yourself to be a fraud and a troublemaker."

Yu Qi replied calmly, "It is not for me to decide whether I live or die. No one lives forever. However, if my blood is on your hands, then your blood will be on other men's hands."

The lord had Yu Qi executed. When Sun Ce's mother heard this, she sighed and said, "Such is the will of heaven. My son will not ascend the dragon throne, nor will his descendants."

Not long afterward, Sun Ce was ambushed and killed by assassins. He died without a son and was succeeded by his brother. Although the kingdom of Wu became one of the three principal contenders to the Chinese throne, it was eventually defeated by the Cao family, who deposed the Han emperor and founded the Wei dynasty.

10

Zhang Jiao and the Yellow Turban Movement

WHILE WARLORDS, MINISTERS, and eunuchs battled for control over the Han empire, floods, famine, and epidemics ravaged the countryside. Starving peasants became lawless hordes sweeping through the land, robbing rich and poor alike. Destitute and desperate, people were forced to commit acts that were against the fabric of thousands of years of Chinese culture: husbands sold wives and children into slavery, infants were abandoned, and the elderly were driven out of their homes to die.

In this social turmoil there lived a man named Zhang Jiao. Zhang Jiao served briefly as a clerk in the provincial granary before he was fired for secretly distributing grain to starving citizens. Disillusioned with public service, Zhang Jiao embraced Taoism. However, the kind of Taoism that interested him was not Laozi's philosophy of nonaction but divination and talismanic magic. It is not known how Zhang Jiao became an expert in these Taoist arcane arts, but the ex–civil servant soon earned himself the reputation of being a miracle worker who could heal incurable illnesses and exorcize evil spirits. Men and

*Talismans of healing, exorcism,
and obstacle removal.*

women flocked to him, begging to be students. Within a few years, Zhang Jiao had gathered thousands of disciples.

One of Zhang Jiao's students was a refugee from north China. The young disciple was a follower of the Taiping Way and gave his teacher a copy of *The Book of Harmony and Peace*. When Jiao read the text, he recognized at once that this was no ordinary book. Attracted especially to the idea of creating a society in which rulers followed the will of heaven and looked after the welfare of the people, Jiao pledged to work toward restoring peace and harmony to his country.

Wary that he would be labeled a rebel, Zhang Jiao initially taught that the harmony of heaven, earth, and humanity could be restored by performing the appropriate Taoist rites and rituals. Shrines and temples sprouted up wherever he went, and within ten years, Jiao had more than a hundred thousand followers.

Zhang Jiao and the Yellow Turban Movement

By that time Zhang Jiao was no longer timid about being a political leader. He declared openly that he was sent by heaven to deliver the nation from suffering and sent his disciples to spread the message that the Han dynasty would be replaced by a new era called the Way of Harmony and Peace. Hundreds of thousands flocked to swear allegiance to Zhang Jiao. Jiao quickly organized his followers into administrators, priests, and soldiers and began to plan to overthrow the Han dynasty.

To identify themselves, Zhang Jiao's followers wrapped a strip of yellow cloth around their heads. Calling themselves the sons and daughters of the Yellow Emperor, they pledged to fight oppression, injustice, and corruption. To the Han government, Zhang Jiao's followers became known as the Yellow Turban rebels, and the uprising was called the Yellow Turban movement.

In 184 C.E. Zhang Jiao believed he was ready to seize the throne. He called his generals together and sent messages to mobilize his followers for a coordinated attack on the capital.

Everything went according to plan until a month before the appointed day of the uprising. One of Zhang Jiao's lieutenants, doubtful of the success of the rebellion, informed the government of the impending revolt. The Han government immediately declared martial law. Realizing that a coordinated uprising was not possible, Jiao made a premature attack on the capital. He and his followers fought bravely but were no match against Cao Cao and Huang Bo, two of China's greatest military strategists. Zhang Jiao suffered a crushing defeat and died of his wounds before he could return to his stronghold. Without Jiao's leadership and inspiration, the commanders of the rebel army surrendered. Within a month the Yellow Turban uprising was completely stamped out.

11

Zhang Lu's Kingdom

WHILE ZHANG JIAO'S influence was gaining momentum in northern China and Yu Qi was attracting a large number of followers in the southeast, another Taoist spiritual leader, Zhang Daoling, was establishing a stronghold in the western region of Sichuan. Like Jiao and Qi, Zhang Daoling was a magician and a healer who used enchanted amulets and talismans to cure illness and exorcize evil spirits. Believing that their teacher was sent by heaven to deliver people from suffering, Zhang Daoling's students proclaimed him the Celestial Teacher. However, Zhang Daoling had no political aspirations. He spent his entire life healing the sick, exorcizing evil spirits, and making the elixir of immortality.

After Zhang Daoling passed into the immortal realm, his son Zhang Heng succeeded him as Celestial Teacher. By then the Celestial Teacher's Way had become a large religious organization with tens of thousands of followers in western and central China. Zhang Heng was by nature a hermit and had no interest in leading and managing a spiritual movement. Although he continued his father's legacy of healing the sick and exorcizing evil spirits, Heng delegated the duties of running his religious organization to his wife and principal students.

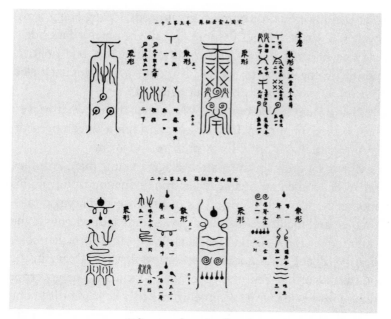

Talismans of exorcism from the
Celestial Teachers Way.

Zhang Heng's wife was a remarkable woman. Intelligent, beautiful, and charismatic, she proved to be a natural leader. Under her guidance the Celestial Teacher's movement became efficient, rich, and powerful. It was Heng's wife who instituted a fee of five scoops of rice for initiation into the Celestial Teacher's Way. The rice was stored in a granary and was distributed to the poor and needy in times of famine. This charitable gesture won the hearts and minds of the peasants, who renamed the Celestial Teacher's Way the Way of the Five Scoops of Rice. Within a span of ten years, the followers of the Celestial Teacher's Way swelled to almost a million. Even the governor of Sichuan recognized its influence and courted the friendship of the Zhang family.

Zhang Heng had a son whom he named Zhang Lu. Legend has it that when Lu was born, a rainbow appeared over the family's home and a phoenix was seen perched on it. Diviners predicted that the boy would accomplish great deeds. Zhang Heng, however, was worried. In his wisdom, he saw the omen's dark side.

"The phoenix is a bird of royalty, command, and political power," Heng said to his wife. "I fear our son may get entangled in worldly power and come to a tragic end."

Zhang Heng's wife replied, "We cannot change what heaven has decreed for our son. If his destiny is to rule a kingdom, earthly or spiritual, it is our duty to prepare him for it."

Zhang Lu grew up to be an intelligent young man. From his father he learned talismanic magic and divination, and from his mother he learned the practices of breath control, yogic calisthenics, and meditation. Zhang Lu was not educated only in the tradition of the Celestial Teacher's Way. Mindful of her son's destiny, Zhang Lu's mother sent him to serve as a page in the household of Liu Yen, the governor of Sichuan. The governor was so impressed with Lu's intelligence that he made the young man his personal secretary. As secretary, Zhang Lu was responsible for drafting Yen's correspondence with the regional magistrates and garrison commanders as well as the imperial court and other provincial governors. Lu couldn't have been in a better position to learn statecraft, military strategy, and the art of leadership. Moreover, his secretarial post gave him privileged access to many government secrets.

By the time Zhang Lu had completed his service under Liu Yen, the Han dynasty was in its death throes. Eunuchs and powerful nobles controlled the government, deposing and crowning emperors at will. Zhang Lu's mentor, Liu Yen, was an ambitious man. Realizing that the central government was losing control of the country, Yen decided to carve out a small kingdom for himself. First he consolidated his financial and material resources by refusing to send taxes to the capital, citing that the roads were blocked by bandits. Then he declared that the governor of the neighboring region of Hanzhong was incompetent and sent Zhang Lu to occupy that area with an army.

Zhang Lu entered Hanzhong, deposed the local governor, and made himself the provisional commander. Historically, Hanzhong was one of the richest regions in central China. However, when Zhang Lu took over the region, he found the treasury empty, the people starving, and the troops rebellious. Zhang Lu realized that for Hanzhong to become prosperous again, reforms would have to be made. Within a month of occupying the province, Zhang Lu announced that he would create a society according to the principles of the Way of Harmony and Peace. First he appointed priests of the Celestial Teacher's Way to teach the people how to honor the ancestral deities by performing the appropriate rites and rituals. Then he instituted agricultural reforms, introduced reforestation, and improved and built roads to encourage trade. Next he reformed the judicial and revenue systems by setting up independent auditors to monitor corruption and government spending. After that he abolished the death penalty, established rehabilitation programs for criminals, and founded orphanages and homes for refugees. Finally, Zhang Lu reformed the military. Instead of conscripting peasants in times of need, Lu created a standing army of professional soldiers.

Within five years of Zhang Lu's rule, Hanzhong became the most prosperous region in China. Agricultural productivity soared, the treasury was filled, the citizens were content, and the soldiers were loyal and well trained. So popular was Zhang Lu's rule that neighboring provinces begged to be included within the jurisdiction of Hanzhong. Even Liu Yen, Lu's former mentor, surrendered his territory. Thus, without bloodshed and warfare, Zhang Lu's territory expanded, becoming a kingdom within a kingdom.

To the Han dynasty, Zhang Lu's kingdom was no more than a rogue government. Zhang Lu paid no taxes and sent no resources to the capital. Even more dangerous, Lu commanded an army that was funded by his own treasury and therefore loyal only to him. The Han government sent several military expeditions to Hanzhong to remove Zhang Lu from power but failed. Armies sent to fight Zhang Lu often surrendered before the battles started. The government then tried to have Zhang Lu assassinated, but Lu's subordinates were so loyal that no spy or assassin could infiltrate his inner circle. Eventually the Han government gave up trying to remove the Taoist leader by force. To save face, the emperor conferred to Zhang Lu the title Most Virtuous Protector of Central China.

While Hanzhong was enjoying peace and prosperity, the rest of China was plunged into warfare. After decades of fighting, four superpowers emerged: the dukedom of Wei, ruled by the Han prime minister Cao Cao; the semiautonomous states of Zu (ruled by Liu Bei, a relative of the Han emperor) and Wu (ruled by Sun Quan, the brother of Sun Ce); and Zhang Lu's kingdom of Harmony and Peace. (Wei, Zu, and Wu are identified as the Three Kingdoms.) Zhang Lu's territory lay between the lands controlled by Cao Cao and Liu Bei and was coveted by both rulers.

In the year 220 C.E. Cao Cao led an army of a hundred thousand troops toward the border of Zhang Lu's kingdom. The prime minister sent an emissary to Lu proposing that they form a mutual defensive pact against Zu. Zhang Lu understood the message immediately: Cao Cao wanted Hanzhong and was giving him the option of a peaceful surrender.

Zhang Lu consulted with his advisers. As expected, the generals wanted to fight, while the civilian ministers recommended surrender. The two sides were unable to come to an agreement.

Finally Zhang Lu said, "I place the safety of my people first. If I surrender, no harm will come to them."

One of the generals interrupted, "My lord, if you surrender, you'll lose honor."

Zhang Lu replied, "If by losing my honor I can save the lives of millions, I'd be glad to do it. What is virtue and honor? Virtue is placing the good of others before yourself, and honor is taking responsibility for your choice."

One of the ministers suggested, "Before we surrender, we should at least destroy our granaries and rob Cao Cao of the riches of Hanzhong."

Zhang Lu shook his head and said, "We have no right to destroy the food because it does not belong to us. Heaven sent the sun and the rain to ripen the crops, the earth gave its soil and nutrients, and the hardworking citizens gave their time and effort in planting and harvesting the fields. Those who rule must honor heaven, earth, and humanity."

The next day Zhang Lu delivered a letter of surrender to Cao Cao along with the keys of the regional treasury and the granaries.

Cao Cao knew that despite his surrender Zhang Lu was still a force to be reckoned with. Hoping to win the Celestial Teacher to his side, the prime minister offered Lu a position in the government. Zhang Lu refused the offer, saying, "I surrendered not because I wanted a reward but because I wanted to avoid war and bloodshed. I place the welfare of Hanzhong's people in your hands and hope that you will continue to care for them."

Cao Cao was a shrewd politician. He reasoned that if Zhang Lu were allowed to go free, the Celestial Teacher would gather his followers and rebuild his power base. On the other hand, if Zhang Lu were executed, his martyrdom would undoubtedly trigger an uprising. To avoid both these undesirable consequences, Cao Cao made Zhang Lu a marquis and offered his daughter in marriage to Lu's eldest son. Zhang Lu knew he was cornered, but refusing Cao Cao would mean death for his family. He himself was not afraid to die, but he had taken an oath to preserve the lineage of the Celestial Teachers. Zhang Lu therefore had no choice but to agree to Cao Cao's conditions.

Cao Cao continued to fear Zhang Lu's influence even after the Zhang family was absorbed into his sphere of control. Lu's followers in his former territory numbered millions. Having such a large number of members of the Celestial Teacher's Way concentrated in one area was dangerous. In the end Cao Cao dispersed Zhang Lu's followers by relocating them to provinces far from Hanzhong. Zhang Lu and his family were also forced to move to the capital, where they were put under constant surveillance.

The scattering of Zhang Lu's followers ended the political aspirations of the Celestial Teacher's Way. However, it produced an effect that neither Cao Cao nor Zhang Lu could foresee. With the dispersal of Zhang Lu's followers, the teachings of Celestial Teacher's Taoism spread with them and took root in every part of China. When Zhang Lu was nearing death, he called his son Zhang Sheng to his side and said, "Our ancestor Zhang Daoling once lived in Jiangxi Province in the Dragon-Tiger Mountains. After I die, you should leave quietly and settle there. Practice the arts of immortality, preserve the teachings, and wait patiently for the times to change. The deities have promised that the Celestial Teacher's line will never fail."

Zhang Sheng followed his father's instructions and journeyed to the Dragon-Tiger Mountains. He remained there for the rest of his life, secretly imparting the teachings of the Celestial Teacher's Way to his sons and a small group of students. Today a descendant of the Zhang family lives in Taiwan as the sixty-fourth patriarch of the Celestial Teacher's Way. The descendants of Cao Cao, however, were exterminated when the dynasty they founded was destroyed by the Duke of Jin.

Part Three

The Wei, Jin, and Northern and Southern Dynasties

12

Kai Kang of
the Bamboo Grove

WHILE THE CELESTIAL Teacher's Way grew in popularity among the common people, a small but influential group attracted to Taoist philosophy and the belief in immortality was beginning to emerge within the intellectual community. This group not only experimented with herbs and minerals to create elixirs of immortality but also shunned social conventions, mocked the establishment, and exhibited wild behavior.

Among these nonconformists was a talented musician, poet, and essayist named Kai Kang. Kang was a virtuoso on the zither. Even as a child he wrote and played his own music. When his family encouraged him to pursue a career as a court musician, Kai Gong replied that he had no interest in performing for the nobility.

"Musicians who pander to the tastes of the leisure class are no different from dogs who wag their tails in the presence of their masters," he said.

Kai Kang left his family and joined a group of intellectuals who followed Zhuangzi's teachings of "free and easy wandering" literally and seriously. Kang and his companions often met in a bamboo grove at the edge of town to drink, recite poetry,

Kai Kang.

and discuss Taoist philosophy. Their outrageous behavior and absolute disregard for social norms earned them both notoriety and fame. The group became known as the Seven Sages of the Bamboo Grove.

Of the seven, Kai Kang was the most charismatic. Handsome, charming, and elegantly dressed, he carried an air of grace and dignity that won the loyalty of friends and the hearts of women. Obstacles did not exist for Kai Kang: nothing seemed to stand in his way, not even ghosts and spirits.

One time Kai Kang was invited to a housewarming party given by a friend. Expecting a large crowd and lots of fun and merriment, Kang was disappointed that only a handful of guests was present. When he saw the host looking dejected and confused, Kai Kang asked, "What's wrong? Have you lost all of your friends?"

The host replied, "My house is haunted. My friends are afraid to come."

Kai Kang was known to be bold and adventurous. "I'd like to meet these ghosts and ask them why they haunt your house," he said.

"You are welcome to stay in the guest suite," the friend replied. "The ghosts usually come out around midnight."

That night Kai Kang took his zither, sat in the gazebo in the garden, and played.

At midnight eight ghostly apparitions appeared. They floated toward Kai Kang, who kept his composure and continued playing.

One of the ghosts approached Kai Kang and said, "You are a very talented musician. I haven't heard anyone play like that in my lifetime."

The ghost sat down on the bench next to Kai Kang, closed his eyes, and seemed completely captivated by the music. Presently Kai Kang finished playing, looked at his ghostly visitor, and asked calmly, "Who are you, and why are you haunting this mansion?"

The ghost replied, "We are eight musicians who were robbed and killed by bandits while traveling to the capital to play for the emperor. When your host built a house on this field, our spirits were trapped. We mean no harm to your friend and his family."

Another ghost floated over to Kai Kang and said, "Our bones are scattered in the backyard near the large tree. Now that you know of our predicament, we hope that you will find our remains and bury them properly. Once our bones are returned to the earth, we can journey to our next life and will no longer haunt the realm of the living."

Kai Kang smiled and said, "I promise that you will all be given a proper burial."

"We are indebted to your kindness," the leader of the ghosts said. "In return, we will teach you a piece of music that has been lost for three hundred years."

The ghosts hovered around Kai Kang and played and sang until the first light of dawn.

In the morning Kai Kang approached his friend and related to him his experience with the ghosts. The two men went to the backyard, found the remains of the eight musicians, and buried them in proper graves.

It was said that after that incident, whenever Kai Kang played the piece of music he had learned from the ghosts, faint echoes of accompaniment could be heard.

At another time Kai Kang was wandering in the mountains singing and reciting poetry when he saw a strange man climbing nimbly up the rocky slope. The man was dressed in a simple hemp robe and had a zither slung across his back. Kai Kang knew that this must be the immortal musician Sun Deng. Eager to learn from the master, Kai Kang hurried after Sun Deng and followed him into a cave. Sun Deng sat down on a flat boulder and began to play. Kai Kang was mesmerized. The music took him to the realm of the immortals, where he danced on the clouds and swirled with the movement of the stars.

When the music stopped, Kai Kang stepped toward the immortal, bowed, and said, "Teacher, please instruct me in the art of music."

Sun Deng responded with silence. Kai Kang was not discouraged. He built a hut outside the cave, settled there, and waited patiently for the immortal to teach him.

Three years passed. One day Sun Deng called Kai Kang into the cave. Kang expected the immortal to teach him the music of the celestial realm, but instead he heard Sun Deng say: "Talent, experience, and worldly wisdom are all necessary for preserving your life. You have tremendous talent but not enough experience and worldly wisdom. All your life you've taken things for granted. If you don't acquire worldly wisdom, you'll lose your life, and if you throw your life away, how can you become an immortal?"

Kai Kang frowned. He did not understand the meaning of Sun Deng's words. Before he could ask again, the immortal said, "If you can humble yourself and develop worldly wisdom, you'll have a chance to come back and learn from me." Sun Deng disappeared into the mist.

Kai Kang returned home. His fame as a musician grew, but so did his disdain for the political establishment. At that time the Wei dynasty had just been toppled. Eager to restore law and order after a hundred years of warfare, the emperor of the new dynasty, Jin, had no tolerance for criticisms of his policies. Oblivious to this change in the political climate, Kai Kang continued to mock the government and nobility with essays and satires.

Knowing that Kai Kang was courting danger, his family tried to dissuade him from making callous remarks about the new dynasty. Kang, however, chose to ignore them.

If Kai Kang were an unknown commoner, the government would probably have overlooked his behavior. But Kang was a famous musician with a large number of admirers. The emperor decided that Kai Kang needed to be silenced. Hoping to avoid a controversy, he sent an emissary to warn the musician not to make further criticisms of the government. Kai Kang responded by composing a poem satirizing the incident. The emperor was outraged and had Kai Kang arrested. Even in prison, Kang was stubborn and arrogant. Denied brush, ink, and paper, he wrote satirical poems on the prison wall with charcoal.

Eventually the emperor's patience ran out, and Kai Kang was sentenced to death. When his punishment was announced, three thousand government officials, aristocrats, and intellectuals knelt in front of the imperial palace to petition for his pardon. The emperor held his ground, and Kai Kang was led to the city gate for execution.

Kai Kang stepped onto the scaffold, sat down, and asked for a zither. The officer on duty, who was an admirer of Kai Kang's, ordered that a zither be brought to him. Kang placed the zither across his lap and played the music he had learned from the ghosts.

When the last note faded into silence, even hardened soldiers were weeping openly. Kai Kang sighed, laid down the zither, and said, " Now I understand what immortal Sun Deng meant when he told me to acquire worldly wisdom."

Kai Kang walked calmly to the execution block and placed his head on it. He was forty years old.

Kai Kang's death was mourned throughout the kingdom. Even the emperor regretted that he had had the musician executed.

Not long after Kai Kang's death, a talented but poor musician named Xu Ning happened to pass by a bamboo grove on his way to a music competition. Just as Ning was wondering what he would perform before the examiner, he heard the unmistakable sound of a zither coming from the direction of the grove. Curious, the student musician searched the area but found no one. When Xu Ning was about to leave the area, he heard the music again. This time Ning recognized the piece: it was the song Kai Kang had played on his execution day! The young student committed the music to memory and played it before the competition judge. When the last string of the zither went silent, the master musician smiled and said to Xu Ning, "It is I who should learn from you. In giving you his music, Kai Kang has accepted you as his student."

It was said that Kai Kang projected his spirit into the immortal realm just before he was executed. Although Kang never attained immortality in bodily form, his spirit dwelled in the immortal realm, and occasionally it would return to wander in the bamboo grove Kai Kang had loved so much in his mortal life.

13

Wang Xizhi the Calligrapher

THE GREAT CALLIGRAPHER of the Jin dynasty, Wang Xizhi, came from a family of priests of the Celestial Teacher's Way. Unlike his ancestors, however, Xizhi was not interested in talismans and ritualistic magic. Instead he was attracted to the arts of longevity and immortality and was an adept in the practices of breath control, yogic calisthenics, and meditation.

Wang Xizhi had a friend named Xu Man who was considered an expert on brewing and ingesting herbs and minerals to enhance health and attain longevity. Often the two friends would meet to share their spiritual experiences and discuss the latest findings of the alchemists.

One day Xu Man said to Xizhi, "I've heard that deep in the Shanyin Mountains in the southeast lives an immortal who knows the secrets to attaining immortality. Let's pay him a visit and see if he will teach us."

Wang Xizhi and Xu Man journeyed to the Shanyin Mountains but never found the immortal. Xu Man returned home, but Xizhi stayed.

One evening while wandering in the mountains, Wang Xizhi came upon a lake, and on the lake were the most beautiful cranes

Wang Xizhi offering his calligraphy in exchange for the crane.

he had ever seen. Xizhi was a lover of waterbirds, especially white cranes. He sat on the bank of the lake and watched the beautiful creatures for a long time.

Presently an old man came by, greeted Xizhi, and said, "You seem to have an affinity for cranes."

Xizhi replied, "You have read my mind. I would give anything to take a pair of them home."

The old man said, "Those cranes belong to me."

"Are you willing to sell me a pair?" asked Xizhi.

The old man replied, "For you, no money would suffice. But if you would pen me a copy of Laozi's *Daode Jing*, I would gladly give you a pair of cranes in return."

Wang Xizhi immediately penned a copy of Laozi's classic and gave it to the old man. The mysterious man looked at the script wistfully and said, "I have heard of the talent of Wang Xizhi but had not expected to see it in person. I thank you for enlightening me."

It was said that Wang Xizhi's calligraphy sprang from the depths of his spiritual practice. His calligraphy was a mirror of the enlightened mind. Simply reading scriptures penned by him could take one to incomparable heights of spiritual experience.

14

Lady Wei Huacun and the Shangqing School of Taoism

DURING THE LATTER part of the Jin dynasty, in Jiangsu Province in southeastern China, there lived an aristocratic family by the name of Wei. The family had a daughter whom they named Huacun. As a child, Huacun studied the Taoist classics and practiced meditation, calisthenics, and breath control.

At the age of eighteen, when most women of her time would have been married, Lady Wei asked her parents for permission to leave the family estate to live as a hermit in the mountains.

"I wish to live in seclusion and practice the arts of immortality," she said.

"But you're only eighteen, and you've never left home before," her mother replied.

"If I am unable to practice the Taoist arts, I'll never be happy for the rest of my life," Huacun said.

Lady Wei's parents loved their daughter. They did not want to part with her, but they also wanted her to live a happy life. After much discussion, the parents and their daughter arrived at a compromise: a retreat house would be built for Huacun in the woods within the family estate.

Lady Wei settled into her retreat and devoted her life to practicing the Taoist arts. The years passed. When Huacun was twenty-four years old, her parents called her to the family ancestral shrine and said, "It is your duty as a daughter of Wei to marry and bear children."

Huacun was a filial daughter. She consented to her parents' wishes, with the condition that after she had married and raised her children to adulthood, she would return to her hermit life.

Huacun's mother sighed and said, "Where will we find a man who would allow his wife to devote her time to spiritual practice?"

Her husband replied, "I think I know such a person. His name is Liu Wen, and he's the tutor of the duke's son. Although Wen is an older man, he is honorable and respects the teachings of the Tao."

When Lady Wei was introduced to Liu Wen, she knew at once that he would understand and support her beliefs and practices. Liu Wen in turn saw in Huacun a remarkable woman whose destiny lay beyond being the ordinary housewife of a nobleman.

Not long after her marriage, Lady Wei gave birth to two sons. Husband and wife maintained a supportive relationship, and Huacun continued to practice the Taoist arts as she raised her children. At that time the Celestial Teacher's Way not only was popular with the common people but also had the patronage of the Jin imperial court. Because the Celestial Teacher's followers were instrumental in helping the founders of the Jin dynasty establish their rule in southern China, they were given permission to build temples and teach publicly. In one stroke the Celestial Teacher's Way was transformed from an underground populist movement into a legitimate religious organization.

Lady Wei came from a family of priests, and Huacun's knowledge of the religious rites and rituals soon won the respect of the leaders of Celestial Teacher's Taoism. She was appointed a supervisor of religious training and was given the responsibility

Immortal Wang Bo.

of designing and developing the curriculum for the education of the priesthood.

At first Huacun embraced her duties enthusiastically. However, the more she studied the practices of the Celestial Teacher's Way, the more she became disillusioned with its form of Taoism. Two problems bothered her especially. First, the Celestial Teacher's Way encouraged its believers to develop an unhealthy dependency on the clergy. Second, and worse, it had abandoned the ideals of following the will of heaven and honoring the earth in favor of satisfying material needs. Believing that the goal of Taoist practice should be cultivating the primordial energy of life instead of petitioning deities to grant petty personal wishes, Huacun proposed to reform the education program of the Celestial Teacher's Way.

When Lady Wei brought her proposal before the leaders of Celestial Teacher's Taoism, she was met with stiff opposition. Disillusioned, Huacun resigned her position as supervisor of religious education and began to develop her own approach to Taoist spirituality.

One day as she was struggling to understand how the human mind could merge with the celestial mind of the Tao, a mist floated into her retreat. The mist materialized into the form of a man with flowing white hair and beard.

"I am Wang Bo, an immortal of the celestial realm," the figure said to Lady Wei, "and I have been sent by the lords of heaven to be your teacher.

"Do you know what is the highest state of being that you can attain through your practice?" Wang Bo asked Huacun.

Lady Wei answered, "From what I have been taught by Celestial Teacher's Taoism, it is the state of Jade Purity."

Wang Bo shook his head and said, "You have much to learn. Practitioners nowadays know only about the realm of Jade Purity. They don't know that the High Pure Realm is above the Jade Pure Realm. In the High Pure Realm there is no difference between the human mind and the mind of the Tao. I have received the teachings of the High Pure Realm from Laozi himself. While meditating in a cave in the Grand Mountains, I heard the voices of immortals. When I opened my eyes, I saw a figure descend toward me on a bed of rainbow-colored clouds. Realizing that it was the Lord of the Great Beginning, I prostrated before him. He handed me a book and said, 'This is the *Great Cavern Scripture*. It contains the essence of the teachings of the High Pure Realm, and you have been found worthy to receive them. Study them well, and when you find honorable men and women, you should transmit these teachings to them.' When I looked up, the Lord of the Great Beginning had disappeared."

Wang Bo continued, "Wei Huacun, I deem you worthy of receiving the teachings of the High Pure Realm." He handed Lady Wei a copy of the *Great Cavern Scripture* and said, "Follow these teachings and you will attain immortality in the High Pure Realm."

Huacun practiced the teachings of the *Great Cavern Scripture* diligently. As her understanding of the scripture deepened, she began to transmit the teachings to others. Her teachings became known the High Purity (Shangqing) School of Taoism, and Lady Wei was acknowledged as the founder of the lineage.

When Wei Huacun was eighty-three years old, an entourage of immortals appeared at the window of her retreat. Lady Wei stepped toward them and was taken away on a bed of rainbow-colored clouds.

15

Yang Xi and the Shangqing Scriptures

AFTER LADY WEI Huacun passed into the immortal realm, the leadership of the Shangqing School went to Yang Xi.

It was said that as a child Yang Xi occasionally went into trances and communed with spirits and deities. Growing up in Jiangsu Province, where Lady Wei's teachings were popular among the intellectuals and the aristocracy, Yang Xi took to the Shangqing teachings of visualizing and merging with the deities as a fish to water. The son of a wealthy family of artists and scholars, Yang Xi was not only the protégé but also the friend of the great calligrapher Wang Xizhi. Often student and mentor would practice meditation and study the Taoist classics together. Xizhi introduced Yang Xi to his spiritual teacher and friend Xu Man, and Yang Xi in turn shared his knowledge of the Shangqing text *The Lumionous Precious Scripture of the Five Talismans* with the other two Taoists.

One day, curious as to how their young friend came to possess this rare Shangqing classic, Xu Man asked Yang Xi, "We've heard that the text is an heirloom of Lady Wei's family and is not revealed to outsiders casually. How were you able to get hold of it?" Yang Xi replied, "My family and the Weis have been friends for many generations. I got the text from Lady Wei's son."

"It's known that Wei Huacun received numerous Shangqing texts from Immortal Wang Bo," the knowledgeable Xu Man said. "I wonder if we can persuade her son to allow us to read those scriptures."

Xu Man, Wang Xizhi, and Yang Xi paid the Wei family a visit. Lady Wei's son welcomed them with a knowing look and exclaimed, "What an auspicious occasion! Having three great Taoists grace my home is not something that happens every day!"

Xu Man bowed, Xizhi smiled, and Yang Xi looked away sheepishly.

"We are privileged to obtain a copy of *The Lumionous Precious Scripture of the Five Talismans* through our friend Yang Xi," Xu Man began.

"The text has given us much-needed guidance in our practices," Xizhi added.

Then Xu Man got to his point: "The three of us would like to receive permission to study the Shangqing texts collected in your family's library."

Wang Xizhi and Yang Xi gasped. They had known Xu Man to be blunt and direct but had not expected him to broach the topic so suddenly.

Yang Xi immediately offered an apology, "Please forgive my friend's behavior. He does not mean to be disrespectful."

Lady Wei's son smiled and said, "No offense is taken." He turned to Xu Man and said, "I admire your honesty and sincerity. However, as much as I would like to, I cannot help you. My mother was instructed to teach only those who have been found worthy by the lords of heaven. Unfortunately, I myself do no have the honor to receive the texts."

The friends left, disappointed. That evening Xu Man called Wang Xizhi and Yang Xi to his home and said, "I have an idea how we could get hold of the texts."

Yang Xi opened his mouth in surprise. Wang Xizhi winked at his student and commented, "Another one of Xu Man's crazy plans."

"Hear me out," said Xu Man. "We are told that the teachings came directly from the lords of heaven. Agreed?"

The other two nodded.

Xu Man then said, "Let us ask the lords of heaven to reveal the scriptures. I know a medium who is adept at communicating with ghosts and spirits. We can ask him to petition the deities to channel the teachings to him. After he has received the teachings, he can give them to us."

Wang Xizhi and Yang Xi were both uncomfortable with the plan but deferred to Xu Man because he was the senior practitioner.

Xu Man approached the medium, named Hua Qiao, who demanded a hefty fee for the job.

The friends erected an altar on a hill, burned incense, and remained in vigil while Hua Qiao entered a trance under the influence of cannabis and fungi. Presently a figure materialized in front of the altar. The friends looked at each other hopefully, but the apparition said in a harsh voice, "Hua Qiao is a man of little virtue and much greed. He is not worthy to receive any teachings from the lords of heaven." A wind blew in from the west and the figure disappeared.

After the debacle, Xu Man approached Yang Xi and said, "I was wrong to get a man of little virtue to communicate with the deities. We need someone who is sincere in his pursuit of Tao. I believe you should be the one to petition the lords of heaven."

"But I'm only a novice in Shangqing practices," Yang Xi

replied. "There are others, including you, who are more knowledgeable."

Xu Man humbly said, "I may have more book knowledge, but you have more virtue."

Wang Xizhi added, "My young friend, we are depending on you."

Yang Xi finally gave in to his friends' request. At midnight on the ninth day of the ninth lunar month, Yang Xi purified himself with fasting and ritual bathing. He set up an altar, lit three sticks of incense, and sat in front of the altar with ink, brush, and paper. Just as Yang Xi entered a trance, he heard the eerie sound of a flute and voices. Xi immediately took the brush and began to write feverishly. Xu Man could only stare in wonder.

Hours later the music and voices ceased. When Yang Xi finally put down his brush, the thirty-nine chapters of the *Great Cavern Scripture* lay in front of him.

Xu Man immediately prostrated before Yang Xi, but Xi stopped him and said, "Although I held the brush, the words came from Immortal Wang Bo and Lady Wei. I wrote only what they dictated to me."

Yang Xi's channeling of Lady Wei and Immortal Wang Bo created a stir among the practitioners of Shangqing Taoism. Unanimously, they begged Yang Xi to be their spiritual leader.

Yang Xi was a hermit by nature and did not look forward to being a public figure. He consulted with Xu Man and said, "I would rather spend the rest of my life in seclusion practicing the Shangqing teachings. However, the lineage cannot be without leadership. I'll agree to lead the Shangqing School if someone is willing to represent the lineage in public events." Xi looked at Xu Man intently and said, "Will you take this responsibility?"

Xu Man understood, and became the chief administrator and official spokesperson of the Shangqing School.

Yang Xi continued to communicate with the deities, recording their teachings and faithfully imparting them to his students. To

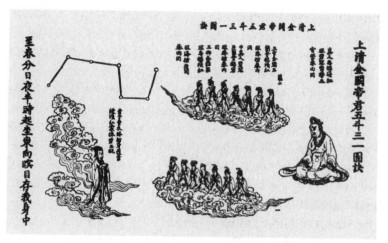

*Illustration from a Shangqing text showing practitioner (on the right)
visualizing the images of the celestial deities (on the left).*

the end of his life, Yang Xi never took credit for creating the corpus of the Shangqing scriptures, claiming that he was only a ve-
hicle used by the immortals to reveal their teachings. By the time
Yang Xi left the mortal realm, the scriptures of the Shangqing
School had grown from a handful of texts to more than thirty
volumes.

The Great Cavern Scripture was the most famous Shangqing text
Yang Xi received from Lady Wei. In this text is the thesis that
the human body is ruled and guarded by deities. Within the
body are two important "gates"—the Gate of Life and the Gate
of Death. An important task of the guardians of the body is to
keep the Gate of Life open and the Gate of Death closed. When
the guardian spirits are able to protect the body from the monsters of decay and illness, the practitioner will enjoy a healthy
and long life. In addition, if the practitioner follows the strict
dietary regimen of abstaining from grains and meat, practices
calisthenics and breath control, visualizes the images of the deities, and chants the liturgies and mantras, he or she will be able
to attain immortality in a single lifetime.

Another text channeled by Yang Xi was *The Yellow Pavilion Classic*. In this text the notion of guardian deities is developed further. The body is likened to a kingdom that is divided into three realms. Each realm is further subdivided into eight regions, yielding twenty-four territories within the body. If the king, ministers, and generals are alert and strong in a region, that area of the body will be healthy. If the ruler of a territory is weak, that area will be vulnerable to illness. Each region is described as a palace or a court. The lower court is the abdominal area of the body; the middle court is centered around the heart; and the upper court is located between the eyes. The task of the Shangqing practitioner is to hold the guardians of the three courts in the body by visualizing their images in meditation.

The Shangqing School is the first Taoist lineage to integrate meditation, visualization, liturgical rites and rituals, and yogic techniques of breath regulation and calisthenics into a unique approach to cultivating body and mind. Although Shangqing Taoism is no longer a distinct lineage, its techniques of meditation, yogic calisthenics, and breath regulation have found their way into many Taoist practices today.

16

Ge Xuan and the
Lingbao Classics of Taoism

LEGENDS HAVE IT that during the Spring and Autumn
Period (between the eighth and fifth centuries B.C.E.), the
king of the feudal state of Wu was traveling in the mountains
in southeastern China when he noticed a series of caves on a
cliff. Knowing that this kind of cave was usually home to hermit
sages, the king climbed up the cliff, stepped inside a cavern, and
found an old man sitting on a slab of rock.

The king bowed respectfully and said, "I have heard that
sages dwell in these mountains. I would be honored if you would
advise me on how to rule my kingdom."

The old man looked at the king intently and said, "Will you
uphold virtue and bring peace and prosperity to your land?"

"You have my promise," the king replied.

The sage then handed the king a scroll and said, "This was
given to me by the immortals. Study it well and use the knowledge to serve your people. But remember, the book will reveal
its teachings only to those who are worthy. If you are found unworthy, this sacred text will leave you."

The king of Wu thanked the sage, headed down the mountain, and returned to his palace. Unsure of how the book could help him rule a kingdom, he sent an emissary to ask Confucius. When Confucius saw what was written in the scroll, he told the king's messenger: "This book is called *The Luminous Precious Scripture of the Five Talismans*. The lords of heaven transmitted it to the Yellow Emperor on Mount Omei in Sichuan. The Yellow Emperor in turn passed the teachings to his successor, who hid the book in a cave on Mount Zhong before flying off to the immortal realms. Thousands of years later, Yu the shaman, the founder of the Xia dynasty, located the text at the instruction of the deities and used its secrets to curb floods and exorcize demons. Before he died, Yu hid the book in a cave near Dongting Lake. From then on, the text was never heard of again.

"Tell your lord that the immortals have given him a great treasure," Confucius continued to the emissary. "If he follows the teachings of the scripture, he will become a sagely ruler and deliver the people from war and suffering."

The king was delighted when the messenger related what Confucius had said about the text. Reverently he placed the text on the altar of his shrine.

However, the king's relationship with the text ended there. He never opened the scroll to see what was written inside, let alone study the teachings. Instead he drowned himself in wine and sexual pleasure and left the administration of his kingdom to incompetent and corrupt ministers.

One day as the king was offering incense at his shrine, a puff of wind blew in from the west, and the scroll was lifted from its stand. In vain the king tried to grab it, but the scroll flew out the window. Just as the sage of the cave had predicted, the sacred text left its owner when it found him unworthy.

The Lumionous Precious Scripture of the Five Talismans did not surface again until several thousand years later. In the third century C.E. there lived a Taoist alchemist, magician, and healer named

Talismans from the Lingbao Scriptures.

Ge Xuan, who spent his life traveling around the country healing the sick and banishing demons. Xuan never charged for his services: if he received gifts of cloth, grains, or gold from the rich, he would turn them over to the poor.

One day while meditating in a cave in the Tiantai Mountains, Ge Xuan was visited by deities who told him that he had accumulated enough merit to receive the teachings of the Five Talismans text. A scroll floated down from the sky and landed in Ge Xuan's hands. As Ge Xuan bowed to receive the text, he heard a voice saying, "The Ge family has been appointed to be the custodians of the Luminous Precious (Lingbao) corpus of scriptures. Teach your children and grandchildren well, and make sure that these texts are used to benefit humanity."

What was recorded in the Five Talismans text that made it so mysterious and powerful? First, the text describes five talismans associated with the five sacred Taoist mountains—Taishan in the east; Huashan in the west; Hengshan in the north; another Hengshan, in the south; and Songshan in the center—and their guardian deities. Each directional guardian is associated with an element and a color. East is associated with wood and the color green, west with metal and white, north with water and black, south with fire and red, and the center with earth and yellow. The guardian deity is invoked when its talisman is drawn. Second, within the text are talismans for mastering the elements, taming wild animals, exorcizing demons and ghosts, and curing illnesses. Finally, the Five Talismans text describes portals in the five sacred mountains where one could be instantly transported to locations thousands of miles away. No wonder the immortals did not want this scripture to fall into the hands of people without virtue.

Another important Lingbao classic is *The Luminous Precious Scripture That Delivers Beings from Suffering*. It is alleged that the deities transmitted this text to Ge Xuan when he asked them to help him steer his students away from self-centeredness in spiritual training.

"You are too occupied with cultivating the Tao for yourselves," Ge Xuan had told his students. "As a result, you can only hope to become earth immortals. If you neglect to help others to attain the Tao, you'll never be able to attain the highest level of immortality. I therefore urge you to work for the spiritual welfare of others. The Tao tends toward goodness, and if you wish to attain the Tao, you must cultivate compassion as well as wisdom."

Ceremony, ritual, and recitation of scriptures became the hallmark of the Lingbao teachings. The more a practitioner performs the religious ceremonies for the good of humanity, the greater the merit he or she will accumulate. And the accumulation of merit is the key to attaining the highest level of celestial immortality.

Ge Xuan passed the Lingbao teachings to his descendant Ge Hong, and Ge Hong passed them to his grandson Ge Chaopu. Ge Chaopu added thirty volumes of new texts and commentaries to the collection of the Lingbao scriptures. These scriptures and their teachings formed a new lineage of Taoism called the Lingbao School.

17

Lu Xiujing's Compilation of the Taoist Scriptures

URING THE SIX DYNASTIES (fifth to sixth century), in the kingdom of Song,* there lived a Taoist scholar and sage named Lu Xiujing.

Legends tell us that Lu Xiujing was born under unusual circumstances. First, he was conceived after his parents had given up hope of having children. In addition, when Xiujing was born, a mysterious Taoist appeared at the gate of the Lu mansion asking to see the child. Looking at the infant, the Taoist exclaimed, "This child is destined to do great deeds. Kings and nobles will seek his advice, and the future of Taoism will be in his hands." Xiujing's parents were not convinced. Their child was neither beautiful nor handsome. In fact, Xiujing had an unnaturally large head and a short torso, and as he grew up, his ugliness became even more apparent.

Xiujing had few friends and did not care for social life. He lived in seclusion and spent much of his time studying the Taoist

---

*Not to be confused with the Song dynasty of the tenth to thirteenth century.

scriptures and practicing the arts of longevity. At his parents' request, Xiujing married and sired children, but after his sons came of age, he left home and wandered off to the mountains to gather herbs and minerals to concoct the pill of immortality.

It is not known from whom Lu Xiujing received the teachings of Taoism. He was not initiated into the Celestial Teacher's Way founded by Zhang Daoling; nor was he affiliated with the Shangqing School founded by Lady Wei Huacun. However, Xiujing was more knowledgeable in the scriptures of those two schools than the clergy of those lineages. Most likely he studied with unknown hermits and immortals while he was wandering in the mountains of Heng, Omei, and Luofo. It was on the slopes of Mount Luofo that Lu Xiujing settled as a hermit. His reputation as the leading authority on Taoism grew, and he was often visited by scholars, priests, and practitioners seeking advice.

One time when Lu Xiujing was in the capital selling herbs and visiting fellow practitioners, a message came from the imperial court inviting him to meet with the emperor. Both the Song emperor and the queen mother were devoted followers of Taoism, and at their request Xiujing consented to stay at the court temporarily to advise the king.

Not long after Xiujing became the royal family's spiritual adviser, the imperial court was embroiled in a conspiracy that affected ministers, generals, and the court priesthood. The crown prince conspired with his sister and a younger brother to assassinate the emperor. They approached a group of Celestial Teacher's priests for help, promising wealth, rank, and titles should the plan to put the crown prince on the throne succeed. The priests obtained from the eunuch attendants the emperor's hair and dried semen in an attempt to use black magic to slay the king. As fate would have it, one of the eunuchs, disgruntled with the small amount of reward allotted to him, informed the emperor of the plot. When the conspiracy was uncovered, a large number of ministers, generals, and nobility were implicated. In his anger the emperor exiled the crown prince, executed the guilty priests, and stripped the princess and the younger prince of their royal titles. Disgusted with the unethical behavior of the Taoist priesthood and the greed of the court officials, Lu Xiujing left the capital.

After leaving the capital, Xiujing did not settle in one place but wandered around the mountains. Eventually he came to Mount Lu. There, on cliff tops surrounded by waterfalls plunging into deep pools, he built a retreat. The retreat soon became a monastery where he and like-minded Taoist practitioners lived and practiced together.

Five years after the conspiracy, the emperor died and was succeeded by one of his more virtuous sons. The new emperor was attracted to Taoism. However, he had lost his trust in the Celestial Teacher's clergy when they were implicated in the plot to assassinate his father. Knowing that Lu Xiujing was impartial and incorruptible, he invited the sage to be his spiritual adviser. Xiujing had no intention of becoming involved with court politics again, but after having been approached several times, he consented to meet with his king.

When Lu Xiujing arrived at the capital, he was escorted into the imperial study. The monarch welcomed the sage and offered him the honor of taking his seat first. Xiujing was immediately impressed by the emperor's demeanor. After brief formalities, the king got to his concerns directly.

"I am a follower of the Tao, but after the attempt on my father's life, I cannot trust the Celestial Teacher's priests anymore. They are corrupt, greedy, and arrogant. Worse, they are power hungry and forget that their duties lie in taking care of the spiritual needs of the people."

Lu Xiujing mentally noted the clarity and directness of the king's thoughts. He replied, "Your Majesty, the reason I left the capital is that I was disappointed with the state Celestial Teacher's Taoism had degenerated into. Its ideals of creating a harmonious society have been replaced by superstitions and black magic. Moreover, many priests are involved in racketeering and extortion and are worse than gangs in the markets and on the docks."

The emperor nodded thoughtfully and continued, "It is for this reason that I have invited you to my court. I need your help. Taoism is in disarray: its practitioners are corrupt, and the priests operate outside the law of the nation. I need someone like you to reform Taoism, rid the priesthood of bad blood, and make Taoist practices respectable again."

In response to the emperor's wishes, Lu Xiujing outlined a program of reforms. He proposed, first, that the original rites and rituals of the Celestial Teacher's Way be revived. Next he recommended that a program be developed to educate the Celestial Teacher's priesthood. Xiujing knew that the Celestial Teacher's Way became corrupt not because there were problems with its original teachings but because there were no rules governing the education and behavior of its priests. Then he proposed to implement a set of guidelines to regulate the behavior of Taoist priests. Under these guidelines, priests would not be allowed to collect fees or obtain sexual favors in return for spiritual services. All gifts and donations would go to the Celestial Teacher's headquarters, and the organization would compensate the priests according to the amount and type of services rendered. A priest or priestess who violated these codes of behavior would be defrocked. Lu Xiujing also proposed that the clergy be subject to the laws of the nation. A priest who stole, killed, or raped would be tried in the courts like any citizen. If found guilty, he or she would be punished like any criminal. Finally, Lu Xiujing proposed that the Taoist scriptures be edited and cataloged into a canon.

During Lu Xiujing's time, the Taoist texts numbered about a thousand. These included classics such as the *Daode Jing*, the *Zhuangzi*, the *Liezi*, the scriptures of the Celestial Teacher's Way, the texts of the Shangqing School, and the Lingbao scriptures. In addition, there were texts that did not belong to any of the above

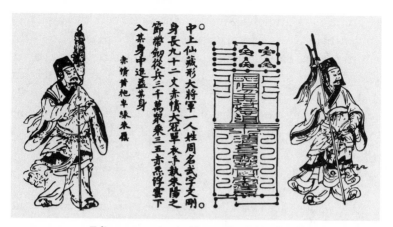

*Talismans associated with guardian deities found
in scriptures of the Celestial Teachers Way.*

lineages, such as Wei Boyang's *Triplex Unity* and miscellaneous
medical, divination, and alchemical texts. Lu Xiujing took the
existing collection of Taoist texts and organized them into three
groups—the scriptures of the Celestial Teacher's Way, which
contain talismanic magic, ritual magic, and liturgies; the scriptures of the Shangqing and Lingbao lineages, which contain their
talismans, rituals, liturgies, and meditative practices; and lastly
the Taoist classics, their commentaries, and the miscellaneous
texts on alchemy, divination, and medicine.

Lu Xiujing's project turned out to be a tremendous feat of
scholarship, for he not only edited the texts but also annotated
them and reconstructed missing sections. His classification of
the Taoist scriptures was used as a reference for future compilation of the Taoist texts in the Tang (seventh to tenth century)
and Ming (fourteenth to seventeenth century) dynasties.

When Lu Xiujing was seventy-two years old, he called his
students together and told them, "I have been in the capital longer than I would have liked. Now that I've finished my work, I
want to return to my home on Mount Lu. Prepare a carriage for
my journey."

Three days after Lu Xiujing's entourage left the capital, a golden halo was seen emanating from his carriage. Soon the entire cab was enveloped in multicolored clouds. When the students opened the carriage door, they found that their teacher had disappeared. Several months later, when the group finally reached Xiujing's hermitage on Mount Lu, they were met by attendants who informed them that the teacher had arrived a long time ago.

Xiujing's students looked at one another in surprise.

"Where is the master now?" one of them asked.

"He was last seen walking toward the cliffs at the back of the hermitage," a servant replied.

The students hurried to the cliff top but saw no sign of their teacher. All they found was a burlap bag hanging from the branch of a gnarled pine perched on the rocks. The bag was the one their teacher had used to carry his simple belongings when he journeyed to the capital to meet with the emperor.

18

Guo Qianzhi's Reformation of Taoism

IN NORTHWESTERN CHINA, during the period of the Northern and Southern dynasties, there lived the son of an aristocratic family named Guo Qianzhi. The Guo family were devotees of the Celestial Teacher's Way and had lived near the northern frontier for several generations.

It was said that even in his youth Guo Qianzhi was deeply interested in the arts of longevity. He followed several teachers who advertised themselves as experts in the Taoist esoteric arts but soon found that they were frauds.

When Guo Qianzhi was about fifteen years old, he accompanied his parents on a visit to an aunt. While the elders talked about family affairs, the boy strolled in the estate's gardens, admiring the dwarf trees and rock sculptures. Soon Qianzhi found himself in a remote part of the garden where few visitors went. Crossing a small stream, he noticed a gardener watering flowers and digging out dead roots. The man moved with extraordinary grace and agility as he tossed branches, roots, and even tree trunks into a cart. Guo Qianzhi watched in fascination. The man had a robust build and a rosy complexion and appeared ageless.

"This is no ordinary individual," Guo Qianzhi thought. "Why is he working as a gardener in my aunt's home?"

Later that evening Guo Qianzhi asked his aunt about the gardener. "Today I saw a servant of yours working in the garden. From his looks and actions, I don't think he's an ordinary individual. Would it be possible for me to ask this man some questions about himself?"

Qianzhi's aunt smiled and said, "If you like my servant, I'll not only instruct him to answer your questions; I'll send him to serve you." Guo Qianzhi was delighted. His parents quickly scolded Qianzhi for being impolite, but the old aunt said, "I took an immediate liking to my nephew the moment we met. Let this servant be my gift to him."

The gardener, whose name was Zheng Gongxing, became Guo Qianzhi's personal attendant. One day when Qianzhi was sitting under a tree in deep thought, Gongxing approached him and said quietly, "Young master, what's bothering you?"

Guo Qianzhi sighed and said, "For days I've been trying to figure out this numeric pattern discussed in the books of divination. No matter how hard I've tried, I can't come up with a satisfactory answer." Zheng Gongxing stood and waited quietly. Qianzhi continued, "Well, this is my problem and shouldn't concern you at all."

Zheng Gongxing then said softly, "Perhaps my master would let me try to solve this problem." Guo Qianzhi was surprised but nonetheless handed his servant a writing brush and a sheet of paper. Without hesitation Gongxing wrote down the solution. Qianzhi looked at it and exclaimed, "All this time I had a sage living in my home, and in my stupidity I have not recognized him!"

Guo Qianzhi immediately went to his knees, bowed to Zheng Gongxing, and asked to be accepted as a student.

Zheng Gongxing quickly said, "Young master, you come from a family of renown. If it is discovered that you've asked a servant to be your teacher, you may be disinherited."

Seeing Guo Qianzhi's disappointment, Zheng Gongxing said, "I have a plan: you should officially accept me as your student."

Qianzhi was shocked. Gongxing continued calmly, "This is a ruse. In this way no one will question our studying together."

Guo Qianzhi replied, "Even if it's a ruse, it is still improper for me to pose as your teacher."

Zheng Gongxing replied, "The enlightened person is not bound by rules and regulations. If your mind is restrained by conventions, how can you know the vastness of the Tao?"

Guo Qianzhi realized his folly. Humbly he said, "Let it be as you have instructed."

For several years Guo Qianzhi and Zheng Gongxing studied together. In appearance the young master was teaching the servant reading and writing. In reality the sage was teaching the aristocrat the mysteries of the Tao.

One day Zheng Gongxing said to Guo Qianzhi, "It's time for you to deepen your understanding of the Tao. Are you ready to follow me into the mountains?"

Qianzhi replied, "I've waited for this day all my life."

Guo Qianzhi approached his parents and told them that he wanted to live in seclusion in the mountains to study the arts of longevity.

His parents were concerned for his safety. Qianzhi's mother exclaimed: "My son, you've never been away from home before. Are you sure you can live alone far from family and friends?"

"I won't be alone," replied Qianzhi. "I'll have my servant Gongxing with me."

After bidding farewell to his parents, Guo Qianzhi set out for Mount Hua with Zheng Gongxing. They found a secluded area, built a hut, and lived there for seven years. Daily, Zheng Gongxing went to gather herbs and minerals to concoct the pill of immortality while Guo Qianzhi meditated, practiced the arts of longevity, and studied the Taoist scriptures.

One day Zheng Gongxing said to Guo Qianzhi, "You are close

to completing your studies. I've taught you everything I know. Tomorrow at noon I will leave for the immortal realm."

Guo Qianzhi bowed and thanked his teacher.

Zheng Gongxing continued, "After my departure, you should return to the world and use your knowledge and wisdom to bring peace and harmony to the country. But beware that you don't fall into traps of wealth and power."

The next day Zheng Gongxing sat on his sleeping mat in meditation posture. At noon he stopped his breath. Guo Qianzhi washed his teacher's body, purified it with sandalwood smoke, and covered it with a muslin sheet. Suddenly he heard a soft knock on the door. Opening it, Qianzhi saw two youths with bright complexions and long black hair. One of them carried a robe embroidered with cranes and dragons. The other carried a long staff. Tied to the staff was a gourd and a fly whisk.

Guo Qianzhi knew that these were messengers from the immortal realm coming to escort his teacher home. He bowed respectfully and invited them into the meditation chamber. When the celestial messengers approached, Zheng Gongxing immediately sat up. He donned the robe, took the staff in his hand, and followed them into a bank of mist and disappeared.

Following his teacher's instructions, Guo Qianzhi left Mount Hua and wandered the countryside, learning all he could about the political and social conditions of the time. What Qianzhi saw was worse than what he had imagined.

After the fall of the Jin dynasty in 420 C.E., China was divided into small kingdoms. Areas north of the Yangzi River were invaded by northern tribes who ruled by force because they could not win the hearts and minds of their conquered subjects. Areas south of the Yangzi were controlled by short-lived dynasties that rose and fell with their founders. Civil war, disorder, and lawlessness were the norm. Public works were neglected, the agricultural economy was destroyed by flood and famine, and bandits roamed the countryside. Worse, the spiritual traditions—Taoism and Buddhism alike—were corrupt, materialistic, and power hungry.

Guo Qianzhi realized that in order to bring peace and harmony to his country, the spiritual traditions must be reformed. While Lady Wei Huacun and Lu Xiujing were restructuring Taoist beliefs and practices in southern China, Guo Qianzhi set out to do the same thing in northern China.

In his travels Guo Qianzhi had heard that the northern tribe of Xian Bei was ruled by a strong and wise king. This king had ambitions of uniting China and bringing peace and prosperity to the Han Chinese as well as to the ethnic minorities. Knowing that the best way to gain loyalty and respect from his Han Chinese subjects was to adopt Han culture, the king was prepared to embrace the laws and culture of his conquered subjects. This plan shocked and angered the Xian Bei nobles.

Opposed by both his civilian and military advisers, the king found himself fighting a losing battle. It was under these circumstances that Guo Qianzhi arrived at the court of the Xian Bei king.

Qianzhi asked for an audience with the monarch, but the request was blocked by unfriendly and suspicious ministers. Realizing that the king would have to be approached indirectly, Guo Qianzhi began to gather information on the court and the imperial advisers. He soon learned that the king had a trusted minister named Cui Huo who supported the plan to adopt Han culture. Qianzhi decided to pay the minister a visit.

Cui Huo was a Han Chinese who not only was schooled in Confucianism and Taoism but was also a follower of the Celestial Teacher's Way. The two men became instant friends on their first meeting.

One day Cui Huo brought up the king's vision of uniting the country and asked Guo Qianzhi for his opinion.

Guo Qianzhi responded, "The ancient sagely kings followed the will of heaven, honored the earth, and were as parents to the people. To unite the country and bring peace, harmony, and prosperity to the citizens, the king must first become a sagely ruler."

"And how would His Majesty go about doing that?" inquired Cui Huo.

Qianzhi replied: "First, ministers must be trained in the Confucian values of loyalty, dedication, honor, humility, integrity, and honesty. Second, the religious organizations must be subject to the law of the land. And third, the citizens, Han and Xian Bei alike, must be educated to view their sovereign as a lord chosen by heaven to rule."

Cui Huo was so impressed with Guo Qianzhi's proposal that he immediately brought his friend to the king. The king listened intently as Qianzhi described the plan to reform the government and unite the country. When Qianzhi finished his speech, the king exclaimed, "Heaven has finally sent me an adviser!"

The Xian Bei king made Guo Qianzhi his personal adviser and gave him a stipend of gold and silk. Qianzhi refused his lord's gifts politely and said, "I live a simple life and have no need for luxuries. It is my honor to assist you to bring peace and prosperity to our people. I only ask for a modest house where I can live quietly and cultivate the Tao."

The king immediately ordered a huge mansion built for his new adviser. It was too extravagant for Qianzhi's taste, but he respected the king's good intentions and settled in the capital. Together with Cui Huo, Guo Qianzhi advised the king on political, military, and spiritual matters. Taking the advice of his two confidants, the Xian Bei king took the Han Chinese name Tai Wu.

Not long after Guo Qianzhi entered the king's service, the politics of northern China took a dramatic turn. The ruler of the kingdom of Da Xia, Tai Wu's major rival in the north, died suddenly, leaving a young and weak heir.

King Tai Wu realized immediately that his long-awaited chance to invade Da Xia had come. He called his ministers and generals together and said, "The new king of Da Xia is a weak and incompetent child. Let's conquer our rival while the ministers and generals are still recovering from the shock of their king's death."

The Xian Bei ministers counseled against war. "Although Da Xia is in mourning, their troops outnumber ours," they said. "Moreover, they are not without leadership. The young king may not be fit to rule, but he is surrounded by able ministers and generals. We need to be stronger and better prepared before we can attack them."

The king was not pleased. He retired to his chamber and called for Guo Qianzhi.

"Da Xia is weak and leaderless," he said. "We should seize this opportunity and conquer them. However, my ministers and generals, except for Cui Huo, all counseled against invasion."

Guo Qianzhi said, "Your Majesty, this is indeed the time to unite the north and bring peace and prosperity to the people. The conditions for invasion favor us. First, the former king of Da Xia was a willful and arrogant man who ruled by fear. Now that he's dead, his ministers and generals will feel leaderless. Second, Da Xia's military aggression against its neighbors has drained its treasury. The troops haven't been paid for months and are ready to desert. Third, the Da Xia people are about to rebel after years of heavy taxation and forced conscription. My lord, all you need to do is to enter Da Xia at the head of your army and the kingdom will capitulate without a fight."

Tai Wu laughed and said, "My friend, you don't miss much." He then continued thoughtfully, "What you say makes much sense. I would indeed like to win a war without loss of lives."

Before the king could continue, Guo Qianzhi said quietly, "I see that Your Majesty's own doubts are assuaged. But you are still not sure how you could convince your ministers and generals of the success of the expedition."

The king immediately said, "You have read my mind! What do you suggest I do?"

Guo Qianzhi replied, "I consulted the celestial patterns and the hexagrams before I came. Both told me that the invasion of Da Xia would be a great success. All you need to do is tell your generals that you are destined by heaven to succeed."

"You've removed all of my obstacles," said the king.

Tai Wu called his war council together and said, "Heaven has assured us of success in our campaign against Da Xia." The advisers looked at each other cautiously. Before anyone could voice an opinion, the king added, "Heaven has given us a chance to be victorious. If we throw this gift away, we'd be offending the will of heaven."

The king's plans for the conquest of Da Xia were put into action without any opposition.

Within a month Tai Wu entered the capital of Da Xia at the head of his army. As Guo Qianzhi had predicted, not only was there no military resistance but the Xian Bei were welcomed by the Da Xia people as liberators.

With Guo Qianzhi and Cui Huo as advisers, Tai Wu's conquest of the northern tribal kingdoms was swift as lightning. Within a span of five years, northern China was united under Tai Wu's dynasty—the Northern Wei.

With the unification of northern China, Guo Qianzhi and Cui Huo became the king's favored ministers, and Taoism became the state religion. Guo Qianzhi was named Royal Spiritual Adviser and was given the responsibility of standardizing the state's religious ceremonies as well as auditing the activities of all the temples and monasteries in the kingdom.

Tai Wu's work of unifying northern China was complete, but Guo Qianzhi's work of reforming Taoism in the Northern Wei dynasty had just begun.*

Like its counterpart in the south, the Celestial Teacher's Way

---

*Northern Wei is both a dynasty and a kingdom that covered North China from north of the Yangzi to Manchuria.

Taoist ceremony performed in Hong Kong.
The ceremonies date back to Guo Qianzhi's time.

in northern China had degenerated into a sorry state. Its leaders were corrupt, and its priests were uneducated and unethical. Taking advantage of the common people's superstitions, the clergy charged exorbitant payments for religious services. They took gold, silks, and luxuries from the rich and demanded sexual favors and indentured servitude from the poor. Worse, since priesthood almost guaranteed wealth and power, entry into the clergy was plagued with favoritism and bribery.

Guo Qianzhi realized that without reformation, Taoism would lose its spirit and soul. Within months of being named the head of the Northern Wei dynasty's religious affairs, Qianzhi brought all the temples and monasteries under state jurisdiction. Priests who had committed crimes such as rape, racketeering, and extortion were judged and punished like any citizen. Next Guo Qianzhi ordered an annual audit of the finances of all religious institutions. Organizations that received income from illegal sources were fined heavily.* He also instituted a system of education

---

*Many temples had been supported financially by smuggling, racketeering, black market businesses, and prostitution rings.

and examination so that only competent and ethical individuals could enter the priesthood. Finally, Qianzhi reformed the Taoist rituals and ceremonies, rewriting liturgies and clearing ambiguities found in existing scriptures. Under his guidance, Celestial Teacher's Taoism entered a golden age in northern China and once again became a respected spiritual tradition.

Guo Qianzhi's reforms were embraced by all the religious groups except the Buddhist sect led by the crown prince who coveted the throne and the priest Xuan Gao who coveted power and wealth.

"The Taoists have my father's favor," the prince said to Xuan Gao. "We are doomed."

The priest replied, "Your Highness need not worry. I can make your father trust you and put us in power."

"What do you have in mind?" asked the prince.

Xuan Gao said, "I will use my magic to enter and control the king's dreams. Your father is a believer of omens and messages from the spirit world. I guarantee that my plan will work."

"What about Cui Huo?" said the prince. "He's a sorcerer and a meddler. It was he who counseled the king to distrust me. He's afraid he'll be dismissed from the court when I become king."

"I will put a hex on him as well," said Xuan Gao.

The following night Xuan Gao put an effigy of the king on the altar of his temple and began to chant. In his bedchamber the king dreamed, and in his dream he saw his father standing over him saying, "My son, you are getting old and tired. It is time you pass the kingship to your son. He is trustworthy and will lead our people to greatness."

The next morning the king sent for his secretary to draft an edict to abdicate in favor of the crown prince. When Guo Qianzhi and Cui Huo heard what the king was about to do, they asked for an audience immediately.

"Your Majesty is in the prime of strength and prowess,"

Qianzhi said to the emperor. "What made you decide to pass the throne to your son?"

The king began to sense that something was amiss. He said to his adviser, "Last night I dreamed that my father told me that I was getting senile and tired and that I should abdicate in favor of the crown prince. This is indeed strange, for as you have said, I am in my prime."

Cui Huo said, "My lord, I fear that this is treachery and possibly treason on the part of the crown prince. I've heard that his adviser, the Buddhist priest Xuan Gao, is a sorcerer who can influence people's dreams."

The king immediately had Xuan Gao's temple searched. Inside, effigies of the king, the queen, and Cui Huo were found, as well as a large cache of weapons.

Tai Wu was outraged. He put the crown prince under house arrest and had Xuan Gao executed for treason.

After this incident Tai Wu's distrust of the Buddhists grew. Cui Huo, angered by Xuan Gao's attempt to voodoo him, decided to take revenge on the Buddhists. He fanned the king's suspicions and eventually got the monarch to issue an edict to close the Buddhist monasteries and execute the priests.

When Guo Qianzhi heard this, he immediately counseled the king, "Your Majesty must not issue the edict. It was Xuan Gao and his followers who were guilty of treason, not the entire Buddhist community. If you execute people for their beliefs, you will suffer great karmic retribution."

Guo Qianzhi's advice fell on death ears.

"My mind is made up," the king said. "I will not have it any other way."

Qianzhi returned to his temple, called his students together, and said, "The time has come for us to leave the capital and return to the mountains. Pack up and prepare to depart in three days."

Guo Qianzhi took leave of Tai Wu. He died on his way to

Mount Hua. His students cremated the body of their beloved teacher at the foot of the mountain. It was said that when the fire engulfed the body, a wispy image of Guo Qianzhi rose from the pyre and floated away into the clouds.

King Tai Wu began his campaign of exterminating the Buddhists. He closed all the Buddhist temples and monasteries and executed thousands of priests. Without Guo Qianzhi's leadership, Celestial Teacher's Taoism became corrupt again. Cui Huo succeeded Qianzhi as Royal Spiritual Adviser, but Cui Huo was a jealous and vengeful man who would not think twice to use his power to eliminate political rivals. Two years after Guo Qianzhi's death, Cui Huo was accused of plotting a rebellion. He and his entire family were executed.

Not long after Cui Huo's death, the crown prince rallied his supporters, murdered his father, and took the throne. He made Buddhism the state religion, reopened the Buddhist temples and monasteries, and began to exterminate Taoism. The new king did not sit on the throne for long. He died of an incurable illness and was succeeded by his young son. By then the glory of the Northern Wei dynasty was over. In the year 589 C.E., the Sui dynasty united China. A period of short-lived dynasties ruling a fragmented country was over.

The Xian Bei, once the rulers of the mighty Northern Wei, were driven out of northern China. They dwindled and became one of the many nameless ethnic minorities living on the fringes of the Sui kingdom. The legacy of Guo Qianzhi's reformation of Taoism, however, endured. The liturgies and rituals he had written and compiled survived and are still used today in Taoist temples and monasteries worldwide.

Part Four

THE SUI, TANG, AND SONG DYNASTIES

19

Sun Xiyao the Medicine Sage

DURING THE EARLY years of the Sui dynasty there lived a herbalist named Sun Xiyao. From childhood Xiyao took an interest in the healing arts. It was said that at twelve he was able to identify all the known herbs and their medicinal qualities. By sixteen his skill in diagnosing illness and prescribing cures surpassed that of doctors with decades of experience.

Sun Xiyao was also an adept in the arts of longevity who brewed and ingested herbs to preserve and circulate his internal energy. One time while collecting herbs by the river, he saw a small green snake lying in the tall grass. The snake appeared to be injured and was near death. Xiyao took some ointment from his medicine case and smeared it on the snake's body. Then he mashed some herbs into a paste and fed it to the snake. Not long afterward the snake lifted its head, as if in gratitude, and crawled away.

Several days later Sun Xiyao was gathering herbs in the same area by the river when he saw an old man wearing a robe of red and gold walking toward him. A child dressed in green was following behind. The old man approached Xiyao, bowed to him, and said, "I am forever grateful to you for saving my grandson's life." Turning to the child he said, "Come and thank the man

Sun Xiyao the medicine sage.

who gave you back your life." The child came forward, knelt, and bowed to Sun Xiyao. Xiyao suddenly realized that this child was the little green snake.

The old man continued, "We are snake spirits who are the guardians of this river. May I invite you to my humble dwelling for a meal in your honor?"

Xiyao consented. The old man took Xiyao by the arm and led him into the river. The moment his feet touched the water, Sun Xiyao found himself inside a large mansion. Inside the mansion, a feast of the finest seafood had been prepared. Sun Xiyao thanked his host and said, "I have abstained from eating sentient beings. Please do not be offended if I eat only seaweed and river grass."

The old man said, "I will not be offended. Name a gift you would like to have. If I can procure it, I will give it to you."

Sun Xiyao replied, "You need not give me any gift. As a healer it is my responsibility to save your grandson."

His host sighed and said, "Even so, I am grateful. For years I've seen you gathering herbs along the river and experimenting with them. I'll give you a catalog of herbs that grow along riverbanks and a manual on how to use them."

Sun Xiyao was delighted. He thanked the snake spirit and said, "I will honor your gift and will always use this knowledge for the good of sentient beings."

Returning home, Sun Xiyao studied the herbal catalog and manual and incorporated the knowledge into his medical practice. Soon he was able to cure all kinds of incurable diseases. His fame as the Medicine Sage spread far and wide. Eventually it reached the ears of the emperor.

The Sui emperor invited Sun Xiyao to be the court physician, but Xiyao declined, saying that he needed time to compile a master catalog of herbs. To his close students he said privately, "The emperor is an ambitious man with questionable scruples. He's not interested in the welfare of his subjects. All he wants from me is the elixir of immortality. I don't think his dynasty will last long."

As Sun Xiyao had predicted, the Sui dynasty fell after twenty-nine years of rule. Harsh laws and heavy taxation drove the people into rebellion. The Sui was replaced by the Tang.

When Tang Taizong took the throne, he reduced taxes; opened the imperial granaries and distributed food to starving peasants; and encouraged trade with Japan, Tibet, India, Persia, and the European empires. The rule of Taizong brought China into a golden age.

Taizong was a follower of Taoism. Hearing that the Taoist medicine sage Sun Xiyao was living in the Taibai Mountains, he sent a special emissary to the healer asking him to be the court physician. Xiyao thanked the messenger and said, "Please relate to His Majesty that I cannot accept the post, but I would be happy to advise him on medical matters."

Taizong formally invited Sun Xiyao into his court. When he

saw the Medicine Sage, Taizong exclaimed, "I have heard that there are sages who never grow old, but this is the first time I have seen one! How were you able to preserve your youthfulness?"

Sun Xiyao replied, "People often learn the arts of longevity for the wrong reasons. Some do it because it's a fad, others because they're afraid of death. I am only a simple man who dispenses herbs to cure illness. There is no such thing as an elixir of immortality. My herbs can cure illness and prevent untimely deaths but cannot bring the dead back to life or preserve the body forever. As for conserving energy and prolonging life, there are no quick solutions. Longevity results naturally from stilling the mind and living a simple life."

The emperor nodded and said thoughtfully, "I now understand what it means to cultivate longevity. Though I would like to devote my life to cultivating spirituality, I know it is not possible. I have a country to rule. My people's welfare depends on me. If I abandoned my subjects, I would have committed the greatest crime in history. However, may I ask you to stay in the court and be my personal physician?"

Sun Xiyao bowed before Taizong and said, "Your Majesty is wise. As it is your responsibility to rule as king, it is my responsibility to be a physician of the people." Taizong pressed Xiyao no more.

Sun Xiyao returned home and began the task of documenting a lifetime of research on medicinal herbs. He died peacefully in his thatched cottage at the age of ninety. It was said that when he breathed his last, a mist entered the room and coiled around his body. An apparition of Sun Xiyao sat up on the deathbed and was carried off by two intertwining snakes.

20

Cai Fu, Judge of the Living and the Dead

DURING THE EARLY part of the Tang dynasty there lived a judge named Cai Fu. Known as the Incorruptible Judge, Fu dispensed justice equally to rich and poor, noble and commoner. It was also said that Cai Fu judged not only the living but also the dead. During the day he presided over the provincial court; at night he judged the dead in the court of the underworld.

One year the governor of the province where Cai Fu lived issued a prohibition against hunting on Taoist festival days. A hunter who had ignored the edict and killed a deer was arrested and brought before Cai Fu.

Cai Fu said to the hunter, "You are guilty of violating the prohibition against hunting and will be punished."

The hunter trembled in fear.

Cai Fu continued, "I will let you chose your punishment. You can either take fifty lashes from the whip now or go to my court in the underworld to receive your sentence there."

The hunter thought to himself, "How can someone be punished in the underworld before he's dead? Only a fool would

The judge Cai Fu with his horse (see also the story of Song Gaozong).

choose to take a beating here." Aloud he said, "Your Honor, I choose to receive justice in the underworld."

Cai Fu had the hunter released. Chuckling, the man went to his friends and said, "Today I managed to outsmart the judge and escape fifty lashes. Let's see what he can do to me in the underworld."

That night the hunter went to bed, still gloating over how he had escaped justice. But the moment he fell asleep, he was awakened by a gush of wind. Rubbing his eyes, he saw two monsters standing by his bed. One held a club and the other a scroll.

"You are hereby summoned to the court of the dead," one of the monsters read from the scroll. Immediately the hunter was bound with ropes and hauled off to the underworld.

When the hunter saw the judge on the bench, he fell to his knees in fear. The magistrate was none other than Cai Fu.

Cai Fu said to the hunter, "This morning in the realm of the living you chose to be judged in the court of the underworld.

I hereby pronounce your sentence: Because you have killed on a day dedicated to honoring life, your own life span will be reduced. The years of life you have taken from the deer will be deducted from yours."

The hunter begged for mercy, but Cai Fu said, "I gave you the choice of punishment this morning. You chose to be punished here in the underworld, thinking that you'd escape justice. Let me tell you this: Justice is dispensed in the realms of both the living and the dead. Had you chosen punishment in the realm of the living, you would have recovered from your injuries in a matter of weeks. Trying to escape justice in the mortal realm, you have forfeited years of your life."

The hunter was drenched in a cold sweat the next morning. Haunted by his experience in the underworld, he tried every conceivable way to avoid situations where he could be killed. He took extra care when hunting in the forest, he inspected bridges before crossing them, he even tried not to get into arguments. Five years passed. The hunter was beginning to think that Cai Fu's judgment was a fluke. "My trial in the underworld was probably just a bad dream," he thought.

One day while the hunter was in a store buying provisions for his next hunting trip, the ceiling of the building collapsed without warning. Although there were other customers in the shop, the hunter was the only one killed.

21

Xie Xiran and Sima Zhengzhen

During the Tang dynasty, in the western province of Sichuan, there lived a remarkable woman named Xie Xiran. Xiran's father was a wealthy businessman who believed that his children, whether male or female, should receive a good education. He therefore hired a tutor to school his daughter in the classics. However, Xiran showed more interest in the Taoist teachings than the philosophy of Confucius and Mencius. When asked by her teacher why she was attracted to Taoism, she stunned the tutor by saying, "I have infinite admiration for Lady Wei Huacun. I want to be like her when I grow up." At that time Xie Xiran was eleven years old.

When Xiran was eighteen, she left her family to search for a Taoist teacher. Hearing that the great sage Sima Zhengzhen was living in the Tiantai Mountains, she made the long journey from Sichuan to eastern China to see him.

Xie Xiran arrived at Mount Tiantai. She met Sima Zhengzhen's attendant at the bottom of the hill, who told her: "My master does not receive visitors or accept students."

Xiran, however, was not discouraged. She built herself a hut

Sima Zhengzhen.

not far from Zhengzhen's hermitage and brought him wild fruits, mushrooms, and vegetables from her garden. This went on for three years.

Sima Zhengzhen grew curious about the young woman who had been sending him gifts of food. He asked his attendant, "Who is this woman, and where is she from?" The attendant replied, "Her name is Xie Xiran, and she is from Sichuan Province. She came here three years ago begging to be accepted as your student. Since you told me that you don't want to be bothered by visitors, I instructed her to go away."

Zhengzhen thought to himself, "To have traveled alone more than a thousand miles is no small matter. Moreover, she has served me patiently for three years without asking anything in return. I've never known such a dedicated person."

"Go and invite her here," Zhengzhen said to his attendant.

When Xie Xiran arrived, Sima Zhengzhen recognized her strong spiritual foundation immediately.

To Xie Xiran he said, "I am a simple hermit. I have nothing to teach."

Xiran replied, "That is exactly why I came."

Zhengzhen was taken by surprise. He smiled and said, "So young, and you already know that there is nothing to attain."

Although Sima Zhengzhen accepted Xie Xiran as a student, he felt that it was against protocol for a male practitioner to instruct a female student in the Taoist secret arts. Several years passed. Xie Xiran learned everything that Zhengzhen was willing to impart except for the highest teachings of longevity and immortality. Zhengzhen began to feel guilty about withholding the teachings from his talented student. However, he believed that if he revealed them to her, he would be violating the rules of the lineage. Xie Xiran understood her teacher's dilemma. She said to herself, "I will travel to the islands of immortality to learn directly from the immortals."

She took leave of Sima Zhengzhen and traveled to the coast. In a small seaside village, Xiran met a kindly old fisherman who helped her build a boat. She loaded the boat with a sack of grain and several bags of dried vegetables and sailed out to sea. Xiran made landfall on several islands where she found strange herbs and mushrooms. However, she did not encounter anyone who could transmit the highest teachings of Taoism to her.

One day as she was drifting along with the wind and the current, Xiran saw a large merchant vessel sailing toward her. Astounded to find a lone woman adrift on the sea, the sailors quickly called their captain to the deck. When the captain learned that Xiran was not shipwrecked but was searching for the islands of immortality, he said kindly, "You are welcome to sail with us. I'm on my way to the spice islands. Perhaps these are the islands you are searching for. You'd be much safer on a larger boat, and besides, it will save you a lot of time."

Xie Xiran thanked the captain and climbed aboard the

merchantman. A month later the ship dropped anchor in the sheltered bay of an island. When Xiran saw mountains wrapped in swirling mists and smelled wisps of fragrance from the forest, she said, "This must be the Island of Immortality." She bade farewell to the captain and the crew and made her way up the forested slopes.

After climbing steadily for a day, she saw a hut hidden among the tall trees. As she approached, an old man came out, laughed heartily, and said, "It's been a hundred years since I had a visitor. Welcome to my humble dwelling!"

Xie Xiran could hardly hide her excitement. "I have finally found the islands of immortality!" she exclaimed. Immediately she bowed to the old man and said, "Please accept me as a student."

The old man smiled and said, "This is not Penglai Island, and I am not an immortal. I am merely one who has attained longevity by eating the fruits and drinking the waters of this unspoiled land. The islands of immortality are far from here and cannot be reached by conventional means."

Xie Xiran was disappointed. The old man continued, "Your teacher, Sima Zhengzhen, has journeyed there in his spirit travels. He would be your perfect guide."

Xiran explained her teacher's dilemma to the hermit.

"His doubts will be gone when you return to him," the old man replied.

Xie Xiran thanked the hermit and left the island. Months later she returned to Mount Tiantai.

Sima Zhengzhen personally came out of his hermitage to welcome his student. Before Xie Xiran could say anything, Zhengzhen said, "It was my fault that I did not give you the highest teachings. Several months ago I was approached by an immortal who told me, 'The Tao cannot be bound by rules and regulations. The teachings should be given to any student who is worthy of receiving them, regardless of age, sex, or social status.

Don't forget that the founder of your lineage, Lady Wei Huacun, received the Shangqing teachings from the immortal Wang Bo.' I was wrong to withhold the highest teachings from you."

Xie Xiran completed her spiritual training with Sima Zhengzhen. She lived on Mount Tiantai until well over one hundred and became one of the earliest teachers of the female path of Taoist cultivation.

22

Luo Gongyuan and Emperor Tang Xuanzong

THE TANG EMPEROR Xuanzong counted several famous Taoists among his closest advisers. They were Zhang Guolao—one of the Eight Immortals—Ye Fashan, and Luo Gongyuan.

One time the emperor wanted to test the spiritual and magical skills of these three men. He invited them to his court and said, "I have heard that fruits are ripening in the southern province of Jiannan. I wonder if the three of you could go there and bring back some delicious fruits for me." Xuanzong deliberately devised this task to test the Taoists' ability to travel in spirit, for Jiannan was several thousand miles away from the capital.

The three men bowed and took up the challenge. The next day they gathered in the hall of the imperial Taoist shrine. Zhang Guolao said to the emperor, "By evening I will have the fruits here for you." Ye Fashan said, "Your Majesty, I can get them to you by midafternoon." Luo Gongyuan said nothing. He simply sat down on the ground, took off his shoes, and smiled. Incense was lit, and the three men went into a trance. The emperor reclined on his chair and waited.

The noon hour passed. Then it was midafternoon. Ye Fashan failed to produce the fruits as promised. The day went on. By evening Zhang Guolao had come out of his trance empty-handed. Then, as the last light of the day disappeared, Luo Gongyuan opened his eyes and clapped his hands. A bowl of fruits from Jiannan materialized in his hands.

Surprised that he had come up empty-handed, Ye Fashan asked Gongyuan, "I was first to arrive at the orchards. How did you manage to get the fruits when I could not?"

"You must have used your magic to obstruct us," said Zhang Guolao jokingly.

"Yes, tell us what your trick was," added the emperor.

Luo Gongyuan replied, "It was no trick, Your Majesty. You see, we were all in the orchards of Jiannan. Fashan projected his spirit out of his body and went to the orchard in his mind. That's why he was the first to arrive. However, while he was able to pick the fruits in spirit, he could not return with them corporeally. Guolao, on the other hand, was able to send a double of his corporeal body to the orchard on his magical donkey. However, the fruits were lost when he mounted his spirit animal to return. I was able to procure the fruits because I not only went in my corporeal body but returned without the aid of a spirit animal."

Zhang Guolao and Ye Fashan bowed to Luo Gongyuan and said, "Your spiritual cultivation far surpasses ours."

The incident made a deep impression on the emperor. From then on he kept Luo Gongyuan at his side as his adviser.

One time the emperor invited Luo Gongyuan to celebrate the Autumn Moon Festival with him. Gongyuan arrived at the imperial gardens and found dancers, musicians, and acrobats entertaining the imperial entourage. Xuanzong walked to his adviser, waved his hand toward the entertainers, and said casually, "These are the finest musicians and dancers in the land. What do you think of their performance?"

Gongyuan replied, "Your Majesty, in my opinion they are

Luo Gongyuan.

mediocre. I can introduce you to music and dance that far surpass theirs."

The emperor was curious. "I had my ministers search all over the country to find these performers. Where within my kingdom can we find better entertainers?"

Gongyuan said, "The performers I speak of do not dwell in the mortal realm. If Your Majesty is inclined, I would be happy to take you to the celestial realm to be entertained by them."

Xuanzong said eagerly, "Then let us be off."

Luo Gongyuan clapped his hands, and both men were transported to the celestial realm. A table with the finest foods was waiting for the emperor and his adviser when they arrived. The celestial musicians began to play, and dancers whirled around on beds of clouds. The emperor sat mesmerized. Gongyuan whispered to Xuanzong, "If Your Majesty likes the music, I can record the notation and give it to your court musicians."

The emperor was delighted. It was said that the music from

the celestial realm brought back by Luo Gongyuan became the official Taoist ceremonial music in the imperial court. Eventually it was adopted in Taoist rituals nationwide.

Toward his middle years, Tang Xuanzong developed an interest in magic and the arcane arts. He surrounded himself with magicians and would-be shamans and no longer met with his Taoist spiritual advisers. When the magicians failed to teach him how to travel to the celestial realm or commune with the spirits, he dismissed them and shouted angrily, "Where would I find someone who can teach me these magical tricks?" The eunuch attendant replied, "My lord, perhaps we should send for Luo Gongyuan. After all, he managed to get you fruits from Jiannan and took Your Majesty to the celestial realm on the night of the Autumn Moon Festival."

The emperor immediately sent for Luo Gongyuan. Gongyuan soon entered the imperial court, where he found the king pacing around impatiently. The moment Xuanzong saw the Taoist, he said, "Teach me how to talk to the spirits and control them."

Luo Gongyuan replied slowly, "Communing with spirits is but one of the lesser skills of the arcane arts. My lord, you are the pillar of the nation. If you are preoccupied with learning trivial tricks of common conjurers, the country will fall to ruin and the people will suffer."

Xuanzong was enraged. He shouted, "Who are you to tell me how to rule my kingdom!" He ordered his guards to arrest Gongyuan, but the Taoist disappeared into a pillar.

"Cut down that pillar!" the king screamed. But before the soldiers could get their axes, Luo Gongyuan reappeared. He floated across the garden and jumped into a bronze cauldron.

"Smash the cauldron," shouted the emperor. The soldiers hacked at the cauldron, but Luo Gongyuan was nowhere to be seen.

Xuanzong continued to indulge in his pursuit of the arcane arts, leaving the governance of his kingdom to his ministers.

Corruption started to spread in the civil service, public works were neglected, and the central government began to lose control of the country. Governors and garrison commanders of frontier provinces ignored edicts from the capital and refused to send taxes to the imperial treasury. Matters came to a head when An Lushan, a commander of a garrison on the western frontier, annexed several provinces and proclaimed himself military governor.

The Tang government hastily organized a military expedition to pacify the rebel general, but the imperial forces suffered a devastating defeat. Lushan marched toward the capital at the head of his army under the slogan "Remove the mandate of rule from a decadent emperor." Xuanzong and his court fled the capital.

While running from the rebels, Xuanzong began to appreciate Luo Gongyuan's advice. He sighed and said, "If I had only listened to Gongyuan, things would not have turned out this way." That night Luo Gongyuan appeared before the emperor and handed him a cloth. On the cloth was a painting of four rivers. The emperor awoke the next morning to find the cloth next to his bed.

He called his ministers, showed them the cloth, and asked, "What is the meaning of this painting?"

One of the ministers replied, "Your Majesty, the painting shows four rivers. Sichuan is called the Land of the Four Rivers. I believe Luo Gongyuan is advising us to set up a temporary government in Sichuan and use the province as a base to retake the capital."

Xuanzong moved his court to Sichuan, where he found generals and ministers still loyal to the Tang. The Tang loyalists gathered an army, defeated the rebels, and beheaded An Lushan. The emperor was welcomed back to the capital.

After Xuanzong regained control of his kingdom, he tried to make amends for his mistakes. He dismissed the court magicians and made serious efforts to attend to the affairs of his country.

However, the damage had been done. An Lushan's rebellion had emptied the imperial treasury, leaving little resources for public works. Moreover, many able ministers and generals had died fighting the rebels. And most important, the people had lost their trust in the emperor's ability to rule.

The Tang dynasty never recovered from An Lushan's uprising. Xuanzong was succeeded by a string of weak emperors, and the central government began to lose control of the frontier provinces again. Toward the end of the Tang dynasty, the kingdom was divided into numerous semiautonomous states ruled by military governors. Civil war erupted, and it would be another fifty years before China was united again.

23

Li Quan and the Old Woman

TOWARD THE END of Tang Xuanzong's reign there lived a Taoist hermit named Li Quan. Not much is known about Quan's background, but it was said that he was immune to heat and cold and lived on a diet of pine needles, nuts, and fruit.

One time while wandering on the northern slope of Mount Shaoshi, Li Quan came across a small cave. Thinking that the cave would be a good place to practice meditation, he swept it clean and placed a mat on the floor. Just as he was about to settle down, his hand brushed against a wooden box. Opening the box carefully, Quan found a scroll titled *The Yellow Emperor's Classic of Using Yin Fire*. Quan unrolled the scroll and saw that parts of the cloth were in tatters. Moreover, sections of the text had been damaged by water.

Li Quan took the scroll back to his hermitage and began the monumental work of copying and restoring it. After he had completed his task, Quan began to study the text, for he knew that the book was a long-lost Taoist classic. However, no matter how hard he tried, the meaning of the text eluded him.

Sighing to himself, Li Quan said, "It is plain that I do not have the spiritual foundation to understand such profound knowledge."

One day while gathering herbs and minerals near the cave

Li Quan receiving teachings
from the old woman.

where he had found the scroll, Li Quan saw an old woman sitting among the pine trees. Before her was a small fire, and over the fire was a small pot that resembled a cauldron. Quan approached the old woman respectfully, but before he could say a word of greeting, the old woman muttered, "To strengthen fire, you need to add wood."

Li Quan immediately recognized the phrase and exclaimed, "You are quoting from *The Yellow Emperor's Classic of Using Yin Fire*! As far as I know, this text has been lost for hundreds of years!"

The old woman replied, "Young man, you are not the only one to have a copy of the book. I have studied this text for hundreds of years."

Li Quan was dumbfounded. The old woman continued, "I know you have found a copy of the text in a cave not far from here and that you have painstakingly copied and restored it. This is commendable. You were meant to find the text."

Quan sat down beside the old woman and said sadly, "If I was meant to find the text, I was not meant to understand it. You see, I've spent the last few years trying to decipher its meaning and have gotten nowhere."

"Then you were meant to find me," said the old woman. "I can explain the meaning of the text to you."

Li Quan was delighted. He got up, bowed formally to the old woman, and said, "Please instruct me."

The old woman and Li Quan spent the rest of the day in the grove. As evening came on, the old woman handed the cauldron to Li Quan and said, "There is a spring not far from there. Go fetch some water so we can boil herbs and nuts for dinner."

Obediently Quan took the cauldron and headed for the spring. However, after he had filled the container, he discovered that he could not lift it. Li Quan searched the forest floor and eventually found a sturdy branch. He tied a large rock to one end of the branch with a creeper and balanced the cauldron on the other. Shouldering his makeshift pole, he made his way back to the pine grove.

It was dark when Li Quan returned. He looked around for the old woman, but she was nowhere to be found. Searching the area, Quan found a small container with a few grains of rice and this instruction: "Boil these grains in the cauldron using the water you have just fetched. Make sure you eat all the grains and drink all the water."

Li Quan followed the instructions. After he ingested the grains and drank the water, his body immediately felt weightless. From then on he was immune to hunger and thirst. Quan returned to his cave and wrote a commentary on *The Yellow Emperor's Classic of Using Yin Fire* based on the teachings of the mysterious old woman. The text was passed on to other hermits on Mount Shaoshi and was eventually collected in the Taoist canon. Of Li Quan it was said that he disappeared among the mist and clouds of Mount Shaoshi and was never seen again.

24

Yan Zhenxing's Calligraphy

YAN ZHENXING WAS one of the greatest calligraphers of the Tang dynasty. His calligraphy not only emanated a sense of tranquillity and harmony but also evoked experiences that bordered the magical. When he wrote about wandering in the mountains, you felt as if you were walking the mountain trails. When he documented historical events, you felt as though you lived them. When he described battles, you could hear the clash of arms and the thunder of cavalry charges. His style was so distinct that no one could imitate it.

Zhenxing was also a poet, a scholar of the histories and Confucian classics, and a practitioner of the Taoist arts of health and longevity. As a young man he received high honors in the imperial civil service exams and was awarded the post of Inspector of Court Accounts. He soon earned the reputation of being incorruptible and within several years was promoted to Chief Auditor. Zhenxing's honesty and diligence made him an enemy of corrupt officials, who discovered that they had suddenly lost a lucrative source of income. A group of them formed a conspiracy to get rid of him.

The members of the conspiracy watched Yan Zhenxing closely,

waiting for him to make a mistake, but Zhenxing was meticulous in his work. They planted spies in his household, trying to find evidence of his accepting gifts, but Zhenxing lived a life without luxuries. Finally their chance to remove Zhenxing came when Li Xilie, a general of a frontier garrison, deposed the provincial governor and made himself military dictator. "Let's petition the emperor to send Yan Zhenxing to the frontier to negotiate with the rebel general," one of the conspirators said. "If he doesn't get killed, he'll be overcome by heat and exhaustion in the desert."

That morning, when the emperor met with his ministers to discuss a strategy to subjugate the rebels, the head of the department of personnel stood up, bowed to his king, and said, "Your Majesty, it is said that a peaceful solution is always preferable to armed force. I believe we should negotiate a surrender from the rebels."

"Li Xilie is arrogant and bloodthirsty," said the emperor. "Who among my ministers could possibly talk sense to this barbarian?"

The minister replied, "Yan Zhenxing is the perfect man for the job. He has a peaceful nature and will not meet force with force. Besides, he's incorruptible, so he'll negotiate honorably."

The emperor agreed. "Yan Zhenxing is indeed a good choice as negotiator." To Zhenxing he said, "You are hereby appointed as chief negotiator. Your task is to persuade Li Xilie to surrender. How many troops do you think you'll need?"

Before Yan Zhenxing could reply, the minister of personnel said, "My lord, if we send a large force, Li Xilie will doubt our peaceful intentions. We should send no more than a hundred guards."

The emperor consented immediately. "You are right. A hundred guards should be enough to protect our negotiator from bandits on the road and not antagonize Li Xilie."

When Yan Zhenxing went home to prepare for his mission, he found his relatives and friends gathered in front of his home. They looked sad and dejected, and some were weeping quietly. They knew that Zhenxing was going to his death.

Yan Zhenxing smiled at them and said, "Why are you so sad? My appointment should be celebrated." He then invited all of those present to a farewell dinner. After several rounds of wine, Zhenxing began to give away his possessions. His relatives started to wail, and his friends wept openly. Yan Zhenxing comforted them and said, "Don't be sad. I have lived a good life and have no regrets. Seven years ago I met a Taoist hermit on Mount Luofu by the name of Tao Ba, who told me that I would not be able to escape this catastrophe. He gave me a little golden pill and instructed me to swallow it when I reach the frontier."

Yan Zhenxing was arrested by Li Xilie the moment he set foot on the rebel general's territory. Enraged that the emperor had insulted him by sending an insignificant minister and a hundred soldiers to negotiate a surrender, he had Zhenxing executed. Zhenxing's faithful servants took the body and buried it secretly.

A year later the Tang government sent a huge army to the western frontier to subjugate the rogue general. After Li Xilie was killed and peace was restored, Yan Zhenxing's relatives decided to journey to the frontier to look for his grave, hoping to bring the body back to the capital for proper burial. Guided by the servants, they found the burial site and dug up the coffin. When Zhenxing's relatives opened the casket, they found him lying there peacefully, as if he were asleep. A bright aura hovered over the body, and on his face was a smile. Even his robes were clean and tidy.

Yan Zhenxing's body was eventually brought back to the capital and buried with honor.

Several years later a merchant passing by the foot of Mount

Yan Zhenxing asking the merchant to deliver his message.

Luofu came across two Taoists sitting under a tree playing a game of chess. One of the Taoists beckoned to the merchant and said, "Are you by chance traveling to the capital? If so, would you be so kind as to send this message to my family?"

The merchant said, "I would be glad to take a message for you. Honored sir, may I ask your name?"

Zhenxing replied, "My name is Yan Zhenxing."

The merchant was shocked. He stammered, "Are you the great calligrapher Yan Zhenxing who died at the frontier years ago?"

Zhenxing replied, "Indeed I am."

The merchant said, "Then the news of your death was false! Your family and friends will be overjoyed to know that you are still alive."

"I am an immortal," said Zhenxing. "Now and then I return to Mount Luofu to relive my memories of studying with my teacher, Tao Ba."

Yan Zhenxing took a brush and a sheet of paper from his side and wrote a message to his family. He folded the sheet, handed it to the merchant, and said, "As a token of thanks for your kindness, I will write a poem for you."

When the merchant read the four lines of poetry penned by Yan Zhenxing, he immediately heard ephemeral music, saw mountains covered in mist, and felt as if he were traveling in the immortal realm. When he came out of the trance, the two chess players had disappeared.

The merchant brought Yan Zhenxing's message to his relatives and related to them his encounter with the calligrapher. At first Zhenxing's nephews did not believe the merchant's tale, but after reading the letter they recognized that the style was unmistakably their uncle's. The letter spoke of life in the immortal realm and of wandering in the mountains and reciting poetry with fellow immortals. They now knew without a doubt that their uncle was living in the immortal realm.

25

Liu Xuanjing and Emperor Tang Jingzong

DURING THE REIGN of Tang Emperor Jingzong there lived a Taoist priest by the name of Liu Xuanjing. In his youth Xuanjing was attracted to the talismanic magic of the Celestial Teacher's Way. He found a competent master of talismans and magical rituals named Wang Daozong and became an apprentice in the Taoist arcane arts. For years Xuanjing learned how to invoke deities, write talismans, and make amulets. Contented with his spiritual calling, Xuanjing settled down to a routine life of writing and dispensing talismans of healing and exorcism.

There was one aspect of their teacher, however, that Liu Xuanjing and his fellow students were unaware of: Wang Daozong was not only a master of talismanic magic but also an adept in the arts of longevity and immortality. One day the teacher called his students together and told them, "My time in the mortal realm will be over soon. After I'm gone you should divide what I have left behind among yourselves. You are free to go your own way or stay in this temple to teach new aspirants."

Wang Daozong died several days later. The students buried their teacher at the back of the temple and divided up the goods.

Liu Xuanjing.

Some took the teacher's brushes, ink, and ceremonial objects, but Liu Xuanjing took only a few old scrolls. One night as Xuanjing was reading these texts, a strong gust of wind blew open the windows of his study. The priest opened the door and peered out, expecting to find uprooted trees and scattered debris. But the winds had stopped, and from the back of the temple a soft mist was seen rising from where Wang Daozong was buried. Xuanjing roused the other apprentices and quickly ran to his teacher's grave. When the students arrived at the burial site, they found the headstone broken into pieces and the casket exposed.

"Perhaps this was a bad burial site," one of the students ventured.

"Yes," another agreed. "I think our teacher is telling us he wants to be buried elsewhere."

While the students were milling around waiting for someone to make a decision, Liu Xuanjing said suddenly, "The lid of the casket is cracked. If we are to bury our teacher at another site, we should get a new coffin."

When the students tried to carry the casket back to the temple, the lid fell and shattered.

"Another bad omen," one student said nervously.

"We should cover our teacher's body until we get a new coffin," a senior student suggested. The acolyte found a length of cloth and was about to drape it over the open casket when he saw that the coffin was empty.

"Our teacher's body has disappeared!" he gasped. "Someone must have stolen it." "And desecrated the grave," someone added.

The students stared at each other in bewilderment. Only Liu Xuanjing smiled and said, "Our teacher has attained immortality. There's no need to get a new coffin or find a new burial site."

After this incident Liu Xuanjing left the temple.

He settled in a small town and began to decipher the texts he had inherited from Wang Daozong. However, even after years of intense study, he was still unable to uncover their hidden meaning.

One autumn day after offering incense to Lady Wei Huacun at a shrine dedicated to her, Liu Xuanjing saw a cave above a waterfall. Entering the cave, he found it dry and spacious. Immediately Xuanjing decided to settle there to practice the arts of longevity. He built a wooden gate in front of the cave, furnished the interior with low tables and reed mats, and began to study Wang Daozong's texts in earnest. After several months of living and meditating in this tranquil environment, Liu Xuanjing's understanding of Wang Daozong's texts began to blossom.

Legends soon grew up around the hermit of the waterfall cave. Even the Tang emperor Jingzong began to hear his courtiers whispering in awe about the immortal who was immune to heat, cold, hunger, and thirst and whose body and complexion resembled that of a youth.

The emperor sent an emissary to invite Liu Xuanjing to be his spiritual adviser.

When the imperial messenger arrived, Xuanjing met him at the gate and said, "I am a simple hermit. My own cultivation is shallow, and I have nothing to teach."

The emissary was duly impressed. He bowed and said, "My emperor would like to invite you to be his personal spiritual adviser. He has high regard for spiritual masters like you."

Xuanjing consented. When Emperor Jingzong saw the Taoist, he said immediately, "Can you teach me the arts of longevity and immortality?"

Liu Xuanjing answered quietly, "Abandon extravagance, minimize desire, practice compassion, and refrain from sexual excesses. These are the foundations of the arts of longevity and immortality."

The emperor was not pleased when he heard this. He had expected Liu Xuanjing to offer him a pill of immortality. Aloud he said, "Can you make a pill so that I can swallow it and become immortal?"

Xuanjing replied, "No pill will give you longevity or immortality if the mind is not clear and the body is not free of desire."

At this the emperor said angrily, "I expect you to do better than give me this kind of nonsense. My alchemists are researching the techniques of compounding a pill of immortality as we speak. If you can't give me the pill of immortality now, I'll wait for their results. You are dismissed."

Liu Xuanjing left the court. Sighing, he said, "Such emperors will hasten the downfall of the Tang."

Several months later, word came to Liu Xuanjing that Emperor Jingzong had ingested a pill concocted by the court alchemists and died of mercuric poisoning.

26

The Patriarchs of Southern Complete Reality Taoism

AFTER THE FALL of the Tang dynasty and before the establishment of the Song, China was plunged into civil war and social disorder. This period was called the Era of the Five Dynasties because five dynasties succeeded each other within a span of fifty years.

While China was plagued by internal disorder, the Manchurian kingdom of Yen was growing in power. Serving in the Yen court was a minister named Liu Cao. Cao was different from other royal ministers in many ways. For one thing, he did not aspire to become the prime minister or the supreme commander of the army even when the opportunities allowed him. In addition, he was interested in the Taoist arts of longevity and spent much of his time meditating and studying the Taoist scriptures. Furthermore, he rarely participated in court gossip and social niceties.

One day while Cao was attempting to decipher the meaning of an esoteric text, he was informed that a man dressed in Taoist robes was asking to see to him.

Liu Cao immediately invited the visitor into his study, bowed, and said respectfully, "Teacher, please instruct me in the Taoist arts."

The Taoist simply smiled and said, "Bring me ten coins and ten eggs."

Liu Cao obeyed, although he did not understand the purpose of this strange request.

The Taoist stood the coins on edge and placed them in a row. Then he took the eggs and piled them into a pyramid. Turning to Liu Cao he said, "What do you think will happen if I gently push the first coin against the second one?"

Without hesitation Liu Cao replied, "The coins will fall on each other, and none will be left standing." Next the Taoist said, "If I take one egg from the bottom of the pyramid, what do you think will happen?"

Cao responded, "The pyramid will fall and the eggs will break."

The Taoist said quietly, "Indeed. The political arena is not much different from this row of coins and the pyramid of eggs."

Liu Cao understood immediately. He begged the Taoist to accept him as a student, but the mysterious stranger only said, "I am not meant to be your teacher. My task is to point you in the right direction. You need to journey south to find a man named Lu Dongbin. He is the teacher you are looking for."

The next day Liu Cao resigned his post, changed his name to Haichan, and began his journey south. He found Lu Dongbin, became his student, and received the highest teachings of the arts of longevity and immortality. Later, while living as a hermit on Mount Hua, Haichan encountered Chen Xiyi, who imparted to him the techniques of qigong and spirit travel. It was said that of all the Taoist practitioners of the time, Liu Haichan was the only one to receive teachings from both Lu Dongbin and Chen Xiyi. Thus he alone practiced the unique combination of Lu Dongbin's techniques of meditation, internal alchemy, and sexual yoga, and Chen Xiyi's qigong.

After years of wandering and learning from various teachers, Liu Haichan eventually settled in the hills near Chengdu in Sichuan Province. He lived to be well over a hundred, and it was said that when the time came for him to leave the mortal realm, a white mist appeared on top of his head. The mist materialized into a crane, which hovered over the body for a few seconds and then flew straight up into the sky.

Among those who witnessed this event was Zhang Boduan.

Zhang Boduan was well past middle age when he met Liu Haichan. Having failed several rounds of civil service examinations, Boduan gave up trying to become a government official. He took Buddhist vows but soon realized that to attain enlightenment in a single lifetime, he had to cultivate health and lengthen his life. Hearing that Liu Haichan was teaching special techniques to householders who begin spiritual cultivation late in life, he traveled to Chengdu to study with him.

When Liu Haichan saw Zhang Boduan, he immediately recognized that this man would be his successor. And Boduan did not disappoint his teacher. Within a few years he mastered everything Liu Haichan had taught him. Realizing that youthful and aging practitioners differ in physical and mental foundations, Zhang Boduan developed unique programs of training for these two groups of students. To young and healthy practitioners, he taught meditation and rigorous calisthenics, and he taught older students who had lost much generative essence how to replenish energy with the aid of a sexual partner. Once the older students had gathered sufficient energy, they would follow the same path of training as the younger practitioners. Zhang Boduan's unique dual-path approach to cultivating body and mind was named Southern Complete Reality Taoism, in contrast to the northern branch, which does not use techniques of sexual yoga. Zhang Boduan became the first patriarch of the Southern Complete Reality School.

Not long after becoming the patriarch of Southern Complete

Reality Taoism, Zhang Boduan witnessed a robbery that resulted in murder. When the criminal was brought before the magistrate, Boduan went to the local court to testify against the killer. The culprit turned out to be a relative of the magistrate's. Instead of accepting Boduan's testimony, the judge accused the Taoist of slander and perjury and sentenced him to a year of labor in a frontier garrison.

It was winter when Zhang Boduan made his way to the western border. A snowstorm forced him to stay at an inn for several days. One morning as he waited for the storm to subside, he noticed a man sitting in the corner, seemingly also waiting for better traveling weather. Boduan noticed that the man was dressed plainly but had an air of elegance. His hair was tied into a topknot in the style of a Taoist practitioner, and as Boduan looked over, the man smiled and invited Boduan to join him for wine. After several cups of wine, Zhang Boduan learned that the man's name was Shi Tai and that he was looking for an adept to teach him the Taoist arts of longevity. Shi Tai, in turn, learned that Zhang Boduan was a victim of injustice.

"I can help you in your case," Shi Tai said to Boduan. "My father is the governor of the province and a man of honor. If you are indeed falsely accused, he will see that justice is carried out. In the meantime, you can stay at my home."

True to his word, Shi Tai brought the matter to his father, who ordered a thorough investigation of the magistrate's actions. Several weeks later Shi Tai brought the good news to Zhang Boduan that he had been cleared of guilt and was now a free man.

Zhang Boduan said to Shi Tai, "I am indebted to you forever. Name a gift, and if it is within my ability to grant it, I will."

Shi Tai simply said: "I wish to become your student."

Laughing, Zhang Boduan said, "If you hadn't asked, I would have offered to teach you. My teacher, Liu Haichan, instructed me to pass the lineage of Southern Complete Reality Taoism to the person who would one day save me from exile and possible death."

Shi Tai received the transmission of Southern Complete Reality Taoism from Zhang Boduan and became the second patriarch. He built a hut in a walnut grove and began to teach the techniques of health and longevity to people from all walks of life. His fame spread far and wide, and he became known as the Master of the Walnut Grove.

Among the many students of Shi Tai's was a promising acolyte by the name of Xi Daoguang. Daoguang was a Buddhist monk who already had a strong foundation in meditative practices when he encountered Shi Tai. The two met on a misty spring day when Xi Daoguang was on his way to the market to purchase supplies for his temple. As Daoguang was entering the city gate, he saw a man striding toward him. The man had a lively gait and was dressed in Taoist robes. When Daoguang could see the traveler more clearly, he discovered that the man had a youthful look despite his white hair and long beard. Realizing that this was someone who had attained enlightenment, Xi Daoguang bowed toward the stranger.

As Daoguang continued on his way, he heard the man quoting a line from one of Zhang Boduan's poems. Xi Daoguang recognized it at once and exclaimed, "You are familiar with Patriarch Zhang's teachings!"

The old man turned and replied, "Indeed. He was my teacher."

At this, Xi Daoguang prostrated before the old man and said, "Master Shi Tai, will you accept me as a student?"

In time Xi Daoguang learned all Shi Tai had to teach. Before leaving the mortal realm, Shi Tai named Xi Daoguang the third patriarch of Southern Complete Reality Taoism.

One time Xi Daoguang stopped in a small town on his way to Guangdong Province in the south. As he passed through the marketplace, his attention was drawn to a ceramics vendor who

Chen Niwan, fourth patriarch of Southern Complete Reality School.

was turning a potter's wheel. The man sang a song as he worked: "Turning circles day after day. Understanding that earth is the lord of the center. Peeling layer after layer until there's nothing left. But how can you peel away anything when there's nothing there?"

Xi Daoguang understood the song to be a Zen koan. He approached the potter, wanting to learn more about this man who had glimpsed the enlightened mind. At the same time, the ceramicist stood up, bowed, and said, "My name is Chen Nan. I would be honored to be your student."

Xi Daoguang replied, "I name you Chen Niwan (Mudball). You were able to encounter the celestial mind because your Mudball Cavity is open."

Chen Niwan left his shop and followed Xi Daoguang into the mountains. He became the fourth patriarch of Southern Complete Reality Taoism.

Chen Niwan met a young poet named Bai Yuchan while

Bai Yuchan.

wandering around Mount Wuyi in southeastern China. Niwan accepted him as a student and imparted to him the teachings that Liu Haichan had passed on to Zhang Boduan, Shi Tai, and Xi Daoguang. Before he departed for the immortal realm, Chen Niwan named Bai Yuchan the fifth patriarch of the Southern Complete Reality School.

Bai Yuchan took the teachings of Southern Complete Reality Taoism to great heights. He incorporated the method of the transference of consciousness at death into Taoist practices and systematized the techniques of generating and using internal yogic heat to cultivate and transform body and mind.

Bai Yuchan was an unconventional patriarch. He never considered himself a leader and did not appoint a successor, arguing that no single person could be the authoritative head of a spiritual tradition. Instead he encouraged his students to train and cultivate according to their potential, believing that some would naturally become the carriers of the teachings of the lineage.

27

Emperor Song Gaozong's Dream

D URING ITS FINAL YEARS, the Northern Song dynasty (960–1126 C.E.) was threatened by a powerful northern tribe named Jin. The Jin ravaged the border towns, carried off thousands of Song citizens as slaves, and threatened invasion if Song did not pay tribute. The Song emperor Huizong was not exactly a competent ruler, but still he had the sense of dignity that he should not become a vassal without putting up a fight. His ministers thought otherwise. Afraid that they would lose their power if the king went to war and lost, they forced Huizong to abdicate.

The new emperor, Qinzong, was barely out of his teens when he took the throne. Weak willed and uneducated in the art of rulership, the young king was controlled by ministers whose interests lay more in preserving their power than in defending the country. Externally weak and internally corrupt, the kingdom of Song was at the mercy of the Jin. In 1125 the Jin massed a large army along the Song's northern border and declared war. Alarmed, the ministers counseled the king to sue for peace. At the advice of his ministers, Qinzong signed a treaty that ceded three provinces to the Jin and pledged a yearly tribute of five million pieces of gold, one million yards of silk, and a hundred thousand horses. Moreover, to the shame of the Song, Qinzong had to acknowledge the king of Jin as overlord. This drained the imperial treasury as well as destroyed the nation's economy.

The next year, when the kingdom of Song was unable to pay the tribute, the Jin armies crossed the borders. Garrison after garrison capitulated as commanders fled or surrendered. The Jin entered the capital, Yenjing (today's Beijing); carried off Qinzong, his queen, and his father, Huizong; and left a note demanding a huge ransom for the return of the royal family. The young prince Zhao Gou fled with his bodyguards and managed to escape capture.

As the Jin armies sped unopposed through the northern lands of the Song, a vast human exodus of Song citizens poured toward the south. Among the refugees were Prince Zhao Gou, his guards, and members of his court. In the confusion of the hasty retreat, the prince was separated from his entourage, and when evening came on, Gou found himself lost in a deep forest.

Zhao Gou looked at the lengthening shadows, sighed, and said to himself, "Perhaps it is the will of heaven that the Song dynasty will end with my death. My father and grandfather neglected their duties and failed as kings. Our family is no longer fit to rule."

Gou was about to submit himself to fate when he saw a temple hidden among the trees. Approaching the temple complex, he found the buildings dilapidated and deserted. As he looked around for a suitable space to spend the night, the prince was drawn to an image of a white horse on a wall at the back of the shrine. The fresco seemed out of place in an abandoned temple, for it looked as if it were freshly painted. Zhao Guo, however, was too tired to give it more thought. He curled up under the altar and fell asleep.

Suddenly Guo was jolted in his sleep by a voice saying, "Get up quickly. The Jin will be here soon."

Zhao Gou saw a tall man with striking features standing before him. The man drew the characters of "Song" and "obstacle" above where Gou lay sleeping and said, "Many obstacles lie before you. Are you willing to overcome them and revive the kingdom of your ancestors? Or are you going to abandon your fate to the Jin conquerors?"

The prince replied, "If I am given a chance to escape, I will reestablish the Song and bring peace to my people."

The figure said, "You will find food and wine on the altar. Outside, a horse is waiting."

Gou suddenly woke up, smelling freshly cooked food and the aroma of sweet wine. He stood up and ate hastily. In the moonlit courtyard he saw his dream visitor standing by the fresco of the horse. As he walked toward his benefactor, Zhao Guo recognized that the figure was Cai Fu, the judge of the living and the dead.

Zhao Gou bowed and said, "If I live to become emperor, I will build temples dedicated to Judge Cai Fu throughout the land and uphold the principles of justice and integrity as he did."

When Gou looked up, he saw that both Cai Fu and the fresco of the horse had disappeared. A soft neigh brought his attention to a white horse tethered to a tree. Zhao Guo mounted the horse and rode away, barely escaping a Jin patrol.

On the shores of the Yangzi River, which divided southern China from the north, Zhao Gou found his bodyguards. He dismounted, thanked the deity and the horse, and was welcomed by his followers into the waiting boat. As the prince turned to face the north and his lost kingdom, he saw the horse rear its legs in farewell. Then, in a flash, the horse galloped into a mist and disappeared.

The Jin tribe overran the regions north of the Yangzi River. However, being warriors of the steppes, they were unfamiliar with naval and marine warfare. Thus they never attempted to cross the river to invade the south.

Cai Fu writing the character "obstacle" on the wall of the temple.

Zhao Gou rallied his people, was crowned Emperor Gaozong, and established what is now known as the Southern Song dynasty. True to his promise, Gaozong built temples dedicated to Cai Fu throughout his kingdom. He also revived the system of circuit courts and judges and set up a department to investigate corruption within the judicial system.

Under the rule of Gaozong, the Southern Song enjoyed a period of peace and prosperity. However, the descendants of Gaozong soon forgot their ancestor's promise to Cai Fu. Corruption, injustice, pluralism, and abuse of power by ministers and generals began to reappear in the Song court. Public works were neglected, and resources allocated to strengthening the country against invaders went to the pockets of corrupt officials. One hundred and fifty years after Zhao Gou had pledged to be the protector of his people, the Southern Song dynasty was conquered by the Mongols.

Part Five

THE YUAN, MING, AND QING DYNASTIES

28

Qui Changchun
and Genghis Khan

Q UI CHANGCHUN WAS one of the seven students of Wang Chongyang, the founder of the Northern School of Complete Reality Taoism. When his teacher passed away, Changchun went to Mount Hua and meditated for nine years. Later he spent another seven years in solitary retreat in the Dragon Gate Gorge of the Yangzi River.

When Qui Changchun emerged from his retreat, he found northern China plunged into warfare as the Mongols and the Jin tribe battled for control of the plains north of the Yangzi. Qui Changchun tried to persuade the Jin and Song sovereigns to make peace and stand together against the invaders, but his advice fell on deaf ears. Both governments were corrupt and their emperors weak and incompetent. "The days of both the Jin and Song dynasties are numbered," Changchun thought. "The only way to lessen the people's suffering would be to seek the ruler of the Mongols, Genghis Khan, and persuade him to rule with benevolence after his conquest of China."

Qui Changchun was seventy-one years old when he journeyed to the land of the khan. After two years of hardship

Qui Changchun depicted in Mongolian traditional robes.

Picture courtesy of the White Cloud Monastery in Beijing.

while crossing mountains and desert, Changchun and his group of eighteen students arrived in modern-day Afghanistan. The Taoists were met by one of the khan's sons, who bowed before Qui Changchun and said, "My father had a dream that a man of great magic is on his way to our camp. I have been instructed to escort our honored guest to him."

Accompanied by the khan's fourth son and a thousand elite warriors, Qui Changchun entered the Mongol camp. Genghis Khan personally welcomed Changchun into his tent and offered him the seat of honor. That night a feast was prepared for the Taoist visitors, and Qui Changchun had the opportunity to experience the legendary hospitality of the Mongolian people.

In the following months Qui Changchun learned much about Mongolian culture. He found that the Mongols valued honor, integrity, friendship, courage, and self-sacrifice. They were fierce fighters but were not the cruel and treacherous barbarian horde the Jin and the Song made them out to be. Rivalries and grudges were resolved in public combat, and assassinations, intrigues, and politicking, which were common in the Jin and Song courts, were virtually unknown. Qui Changchun also noticed, however, that the virtues of compassion and filial gratitude toward elders were sadly lacking among these nomads of the steppes. The old and weak were abandoned when they could not keep up with the rest of the tribe, and gentleness and sensitivity in men were equated with cowardice.

Qui Changchun thought to himself, "If the Mongols are to unite and rule China, they must develop filial gratitude, respect, and tolerance. Resolving conflicts through personal combat may work for a nomadic tribe, but once these warriors settle in cities and rule a sedentary nation, they will need to learn to establish and operate a judicial system. I must find a way to teach the khan and his successors the art of benevolent governance and statecraft."

Qui Changchun's chance came when a violent summer storm hit the Mongol camp. Winds destroyed yurts and lightning killed humans and livestock. The khan paced around in his tent, frustrated and angry. "I am the Great Khan," he shouted. "I've won a hundred battles, and yet against this storm I can do nothing." By his side, his fourth son, the one who had escorted Qui Changchun into the Mongol camp, said, "The Taoist is a man of power. Perhaps he can banish the storm."

Genghis Khan quickly summoned Qui Changchun to his tent and said, "I am told that Taoists have power over the elements. Please banish this storm and save my people."

Qui Changchun set up an altar in the khan's yurt, lit seven candles and positioned them in the pattern of the Big Dipper, and chanted words of power. Immediately the thunder and lightning ceased and the winds died.

The khan bowed before Changchun and said, "Truly you are a man of great magic. We Mongols believe that violent storms are messages from the spirits. Do you know what the spirits are trying to tell me?"

Qui Changchun saw that his chance for educating the khan had come. He replied, "We Han Chinese also believe that storms carry messages from the deities. This storm, Great Khan, is a warning. The spirits are telling you that without the virtues of compassion, tolerance, and filial gratitude, you are nothing but a violent force destroying everything in your path. You may become a great conqueror, but after the conquest, only smoke and ruin will be left."

The khan was impressed. To Changchun he said, "I will do as the great spirits have instructed. From now on you will stay by my side and be my adviser."

Qui Changchun became Genghis Khan's adviser and friend. The Taoist introduced the Khan to the *Daode Jing* and the virtues of filial gratitude, respect, compassion, and tolerance. Often the khan was accompanied by his third and fourth sons, who listened attentively.

Summer and autumn passed. When the first snows arrived, the Mongols were comfortably settled in their winter camp. One day Genghis Khan and Qui Changchun were enjoying cups of warm wine when the khan looked intently at his adviser and said, "I've been thinking a lot lately about succession. I have five sons, all of whom are worthy to be the next khan. I want your honest opinion as to which son would be the best candidate to succeed me."

Qui Changchun pondered and said slowly, "Your eldest son is a great warrior. He is equally adept at fighting on horseback and on foot. No one can match his skill with the bow, the sword, and the spear."

The khan nodded and said, "You have a keen eye. I like this son very much. He's loyal and brave and is always the first to rush into battle."

"It is for this reason that your eldest son is not a suitable successor," Changchun said. "A great khan should not only be a powerful warrior but also be skilled in strategy and leadership.

This man is best suited as the general of the vanguard army. He will open the way for your conquest even if it means sacrificing his life."*

"How about my second son?" asked the khan.

Qui Changchun replied, "Your second son is a follower, not a leader. He may not be as intelligent as the others, but he'll do whatever his lord bids him, even at the cost of his name and reputation."†

The khan smiled and said, "You have read my thoughts."

Both men were silent for a long time. Then Qui Changchun said, "Your third son has learned much about virtue and benevolent kingship. He respects the abilities of his peers and subordinates and knows how to evaluate advice given to him. Decisive in action and calm in the midst of crisis, he sees the unification of China not as a glorious conquest but as an end to war and suffering."

Genghis Khan was impressed by Qui Changchun's observations. "It has been my wish to appoint Kublai as successor. Your confirmation has strengthened my resolve to pass the kingship to him."‡

"Although I've now chosen my successor," the khan continued, "I'd like to hear what you have to say about my two youngest sons."

Changchun replied, "Don't belittle your fourth son because he has a gentle spirit and a kind heart. He may not lead warriors

---

*The eldest son of Genghis Khan led the Mongol armies into China. He died in battle but not before suffering more than a hundred wounds.

†The second son of Genghis Khan took on the task of pacifying Mongol warlords who opposed his brother emperor's decision to recruit Han Chinese into his service. "Better for me than you to be unpopular," he had said to his brother.

‡Genghis Khan's third son succeeded him as the next khan. Kublai Khan defeated both the Jin and the Southern Song and became the first emperor of the Yuan dynasty.

into battle, but one day his sense of filial duty will save your life."*

Qui Changchun continued, "As for your youngest son, what he lacks in strength is fully compensated for by intelligence. He is a gifted strategist, statesman, and diplomat. If Kublai is to succeed, he must have the support of his youngest brother."†

Genghis Khan was so appreciative of Qui Changchun's advice that he invited the Taoist to remain with him as his adviser.

But Changchun said, "My work here is done. I have succeeded in finding a true leader who can unite China and put an end to civil war. I plan to leave in the spring when the paths are clear of snow. I don't think we'll meet again."

Qui Changchun left the Mongol camp with the arrival of spring. He and his students made the two-year trek back to Yenjing, the capital of the Jin dynasty.

In the year 1234 the victorious Mongol armies entered the Jin capital. In 1279 the Southern Song capitulated, and China was united under the Yuan dynasty of the Mongols.

By then Qui Changchun had founded the Dragon Gate (Longmen) branch of Northern Complete Reality Taoism and was living in a small rundown monastery named Eternal Heaven Temple in Yenjing. Years of warfare and neglect had left the monastery in disrepair. When Kublai Khan entered Yenjing, he decreed that the monastery be renovated and expanded. The monastery was renamed White Cloud Monastery, and Qui Changchun became its abbot. Today White Cloud Monastery

---

*It was said that when Genghis Khan was gravely ill, his fourth son offered his life to the spirits in exchange for his father's. The khan recovered, but his son died.

†The fifth son of Genghis Khan became a close adviser to Kublai Khan. He served as military strategist in the Mongols' conquest of China and became an influential cabinet minister after the establishment of the Yuan dynasty.

is the headquarters of the Dragon Gate School as well as the Chinese Taoist Association.

When Qui Changchun was eighty-one years old, he called his students together and said, "I was told by my teacher Wang Chongyang and my Taoist brother Ma Danyang that when the teachings of the Complete Reality School were established in China, I would be free to leave the mortal realm. I have lived to see that day. My work is over, and I leave you the legacy of continuing the lineage."

Qui Changchun sat in meditation posture, closed his eyes, and projected his spirit into the immortal realm.

29

The Compilation
of the Taoist Canon

ZHANG YUCHU WAS the forty-third patriarch of the Celestial Teacher's Way. His bloodline and lineage could be traced back to Zhang Daoling, the founder of that school in the third century.

The emperor who established the Ming dynasty (1368–1644), Zhu Yuanchang, was a strong believer in Taoist magic. It was said that he had the help of Taoist magicians and diviners in defeating the Yuan dynasty of the Mongols. Since the Celestial Teacher's Way was the premier Taoist sect specializing in ritualistic and talismanic magic, the emperor invited Zhang Yuchu to be Supervisor of Religious Affairs in his kingdom.

After several years of service, Yuchu soon discovered that his emperor did not really care about learning the Taoist arts of cultivating body and mind. All Yuanchang wanted was to have powerful magicians by his side to protect him. Although Zhang Yuchu was disappointed, he knew he had to maintain the appearance of attending to his emperor's wishes. Advisers who disagreed with Yuanchang often disappeared without a trace.

Although Zhang Yuchu presided over Taoist ceremonies in

Zhang Yuchu at work compiling the Taoist Canon.

the court and was the head of all the temples and monasteries, he spent most of his time poring over Taoist texts that had been collected over the centuries. Talented as a scholar and gifted in editorial skills, Yuchu quickly realized that the Taoist scriptures needed to be compiled and cataloged. The last compilation of a Taoist canon had occurred during the Tang dynasty, which was almost a thousand years earlier. When Yuchu examined the existing corpus of the Taoist scriptures, he found that some had variant editions, others had copy errors, and many had missing sections. Most important, texts that were written after the previous compilation of the canon were neither collected nor cataloged. Zhang Yuchu decided to make the new compilation of the Taoist scriptures his life's work.

In the meantime trouble was brewing within the Ming court. Zhu Yuanchang had died and was succeeded by his grandson Weidi. Naive and gullible, the young emperor relied on his royal uncles' advice on ruling the country. The most powerful imperial relative advising Weidi was his fourth uncle, the Duke of Yen, who was not only the supreme commander of the army but also the most influential minister on the king's cabinet. The duke had been the favorite son of the first Ming emperor and would have succeeded as ruler if Zhu Yuanchang had not lost his mind in his old age. Instead of passing the kingship to his most able son, the senile and paranoid emperor decided to make his grandson the successor. Angry that his right to kingship was given to a young upstart, the duke bided his time, knowing that sooner or later the boy emperor would discredit himself and be forced to abdicate.

Although the Mongols had been defeated and pushed back to Central Asia, the Ming dynasty was still threatened by aggressive tribal kingdoms in the northeast. During the second year of Weidi's reign, the Duke of Yen was appointed general of the Northern Expedition and was charged with pacifying the tribes that blocked the trade route to Korea. The duke won a resounding victory and was welcomed back to the capital as a conquering hero. The emperor, jealous of his uncle's popularity, decided that he would match the duke's heroic feats by personally leading an army to conquer the small tribal kingdom of Qi. However, unlike his uncle, the emperor was not a military leader. Weidi suffered a devastating defeat and was pursued by the Qi army all the way back to his capital. An urgent message was sent to the Duke of Yen begging him to rescue the emperor from the barbarian horde. The duke saw that his chance to seize the throne had come. He gathered a large army, defeated the Qi troops, and entered the capital once again as the national hero. On the night of the victory celebrations, a fire broke out in the palace. Before the flames could be extinguished, the king's chamber was burned to ashes. Weidi, his queen, and his principal concubines were never found. The investigators of the incident (who were appointed by the duke) concluded that the fire was an accident.

The case was closed after several servants were named as culprits and executed for carelessness.

The Duke of Yen was crowned as the new Ming emperor. The new emperor took the name Yong Li and ushered in a reign of peace and prosperity. Yong Li was an unusual man. He was cunning and ruthless but also virtuous in many ways. He had no qualms about using questionable means to seize the throne, but once he became emperor, he attended to the welfare of his subjects. Yong Li opened trade routes to Europe, reformed the taxation system to minimize corruption, and began massive public works of flood prevention and reforestation. A believer in religious freedom, he endowed Taoist, Buddhist, Islamic, and Christian temples alike.

Because of his status in the Ming court, Zhang Yuchu received imperial patronage in his monumental task of compiling the new Taoist canon. At the height of Yong Li's reign, Yuchu had several hundred assistants copying and cataloging some six thousand volumes of Taoist scriptures. The final decisions on resolving major inconsistencies from variant editions, however, were made by Zhang Yuchu and a small circle of Taoist scholars.

The work of compiling the Taoist canon continued after the death of Emperor Yong Li and Celestial Teacher Zhang Yuchu. In 1445, during the reign of Zheng Tong, the compilation of the Taoist canon was completed. It contained 5,305 texts and was divided into the following sections: Spirit Cavern, which consists primarily of the Shangqing scriptures; Mysterious Cavern, which consists primarily of the Lingbao scriptures; Great Mystery, which consists primarily of internal-alchemical texts; Great Clarity, which consists of non-Taoist texts, including the military classic *Sunzi;* and the Standard Orthodox, which contains scriptures of the Celestial Teacher's Way. Woodblocks of the texts were painstakingly carved, and the new Taoist canon was printed and distributed. Because the canon was published during the reign of Zheng Tong, it was called the Zheng Tong Taoist canon. A hundred years later, more texts were added to the canon, and an addendum titled the Wan Li canon was published during the reign of the Ming emperor Wan Li (1573–1619).

Both canons have been preserved to this day. One set of the original woodblocks is stored at White Cloud Monastery in Beijing and another set is kept at Blue Sheep Monastery in Chengdu.

30

Lou Jinhuan and Emperor Yongzheng

THE MANCHURIANS WHO founded the Qing dynasty (1644–1911) were Buddhists. However, after their conquest of China, they realized that to win the respect of the Han Chinese majority they had to adopt Confucianism, and to prevent discontent from fermenting in the general population they had to honor Taoism.

The third emperor of the Qing dynasty, Yongzheng, was a devout Buddhist who had a peripheral interest in Taoism. In the ninth year of his reign, the emperor fell seriously ill. When the court physicians could neither diagnose nor cure the illness, Yongzheng consented to consult with a Taoist priest named Jia Shifang, who had a reputation for curing strange diseases.

The priest Jia Shifang was brought to the palace to examine the king. Shifang entered the emperor's bedchamber, examined his patient, and pronounced confidently: "Your Majesty's illness is the consequence of the tax and agrarian reforms. The guardians of your body are in turmoil because heaven and earth are

Lou Jinhuan writing talismans of exorcism outside Emperor Yongzheng's bedchamber.

not in their proper places.* If you rescind the orders, the deities will the placated, and you will recover."

When Yongzheng had inherited the throne from his father, the treasury was empty. Corruption in the revenue department and the exemption of the Manchurian nobility from land tax were the main causes of a growing national deficit. This led to dire consequences: there were no emergency funds for flood and famine relief and no resources for public works. Worse, the Qing government could hardly pay its soldiers. To remedy the situation, Yongzheng decided to institute a graduated scale of taxation, with the nobility bearing the brunt of the taxes. The tax reforms filled the coffers of the national treasury but made Yongzheng extremely unpopular with the Manchurian aristocrats. It was not uncommon to see tax collectors arriving at the estates of the nobility with a contingent of imperial guards. In

*Meaning that the nobles were brought down to commoner status as far as taxation was concerned.

addition Yongzheng dismissed several powerful nobles from his cabinet on charges of pluralism and corruption and also established a council of auditors directly answerable to him.

Thus when the nobles heard that Yongzheng was about to consult with the priest-healer Jia Shifang about his illness, they bribed the priest to convince the emperor that the political reforms had angered the deities. The conspirators believed they had nothing to lose. If Jia Shifang succeeded, the reforms would be rescinded; if the priest failed, he would take the blame. They figured that the emperor was so weak from his illness that he would accept any advice that could help him recover. However, they grossly underestimated their emperor: Yongzheng was one of the most intelligent and cunning monarchs to sit on the Qing throne. When the emperor heard Jia Shifang's words, he became suspicious.

Yongzheng called his thirteenth brother, who was the head of the department of intelligence, and said, "Find out all you can about the priest Jia Shifang. Have his movements watched. I suspect he is in league with those who are opposing my reforms."

As the emperor had expected, Jia Shifang was seen visiting influential nobles in the capital. Spies planted in the noble houses also reported that Shifang had been promised vast amounts of gold and silk should he succeed in convincing the emperor to abolish the reforms.

Yongzheng had Jia Shifang arrested and executed for treason. The nobles involved in the plot were exiled or stripped of their titles.

After this incident Yongzheng's illness went from bad to worse. His youngest son, a follower of the Celestial Teacher's Way, approached his father and said, "I believe that Jia Shifang did more than deceive you. Most likely he wove a spell that was intended to kill you."

Yongzheng was alarmed. His son continued, "I know that the priests of the Celestial Teacher's Way are experts in exorcism and talismanic magic. I think we should get their help."

Yongzheng was not a believer of talismanic magic, but with all possible options of cure exhausted, he accepted his son's advice.

On Dragon-Tiger Mountain, in the principal temple of the Celestial Teacher's Way in southeastern China, there lived a low-ranking priest named Lou Jinhuan. When the emperor's summons arrived at the temple, the senior priests were reluctant to accept the task of banishing the evil aura afflicting the emperor, fearing that they would be executed should they fail. However, the emperor's summons could not be ignored, so they appointed Lou Jinhuan to take care of Yongzheng's problem. Jinhuan had no ambitions of climbing the ecclesiastical ladder and would probably have lived out his life doing small chores in the temple if he had not been summoned to the capital.

When Lou Jinhuan arrived at the palace and saw Yongzheng's condition, he realized without a doubt that the emperor was being attacked by an evil spell. He immediately set up an altar outside the king's bedchamber and performed the magic of exorcism.

Three days later Yongzheng miraculously recovered. As a result of his work, Lou Jinhuan the low-ranking priest became a royal spiritual adviser, and the Celestial Teacher's School was given favored status throughout the country. Yongzheng even had a monument erected on Dragon-Tiger Mountain to commemorate his miraculous recovery.

Lou Jinhuan turned out to be an extraordinary man. Knowing that his emperor was at heart a Buddhist, he never discussed Taoist teachings in Yongzheng's presence and did not try to promote Taoism in the Qing court. Unassuming and lacking personal and political ambitions, Lou Jinhuan gained Yongzheng's trust and friendship and eventually became the tutor to the emperor's youngest son.

It was from Lou Jinhuan that Yongzheng's third son learned about the Taoist principles of contentment and yielding. In the end the prince's Taoist training would save his life.

Lou Jinhuan and Emperor Yongzheng

Yongzheng's succession was plagued with intrigue and rivalry between his eldest and second sons. Of the three princes, the first was a ruthless politician, the second a consummate diplomat, and the third a brilliant thinker. Yongzheng himself was an observant man and knew that each prince was worthy of the throne in his own way: the eldest would rule by power, the second by guile, and the third by benevolence.

In the final years of Yongzheng's life, the eldest prince conspired to assassinate the second prince, whom he believed was the chief rival to the throne. The attempt failed, and the emperor gave his eldest son the honor of committing suicide. Afterward the emperor discovered that his second son had tricked his elder brother into conspiracy by planting rumors that Yongzheng had no intention of passing the throne to the eldest prince.

Disappointed, the aging emperor summoned his youngest son to discuss the matter of succession. When the royal emissary arrived at the prince's home, he found the prince lying in a coffin playing dead and his tutor Lou Jinhuan performing the last rites.

When the messenger reported the incident to the emperor, Yongzheng sighed and said, "I understand this boy completely. He's trying to tell me that he'll be a dead man if I give him the throne. Such wisdom at a young age! I will appoint my second son, Qianlong, to succeed me. In a court plagued with intrigues, perhaps he's the best choice after all."

Qianlong succeeded Yongzheng to become one of most powerful emperors of the Qing dynasty. His younger brother never entered the political arena. Shunning cabinet posts, military commands, and even titles of duke and marquis, the third son of Yongzheng lived a comfortable and long life delighting in the company of his Taoist and Buddhist friends.